VINTAGE Camper Trailer COOKBOOK

VINTAGE
Camper Trailer
COOKBOOK

PAUL LACITINOLA *and* CAROLINE LACITINOLA

Gibbs Smith

First Edition
30 29 28 27 26 5 4 3 2 1

Thanks to the following for their help with the vintage photographs and postcards included in the book: Phil Noyes at Trailerama who shared images from his private collection, Johnny Agnew and Steven Butcher from Funky Junk Farms, Brian Hart at UNC Asheville, Scott Burud, and Glenn Jensen. We also thank the following companies: The Curt Teich Collection, The Asheville Postcard Company, and The Tichnore Brothers Collection, Boston Public Library.

Published by
Gibbs Smith
570 N. Sportsplex Drive
Kaysville, Utah 84037
www.gibbs-smith.com
The authorized representative in the EEA is Simon and Schuster Netherlands BV, Herculesplein 96 3584 AA Utrecht, Netherlands, info@simonandschuster.nl

Designed by Sheryl Dickert
Printed and bound in China

This product is made of FSC®-certified and other controlled material.

FSC www.fsc.org MIX Paper | Supporting responsible forestry FSC® C144853

Library of Congress Control Number: 2025938531
ISBN: 978-1-4236-6884-8

Contents

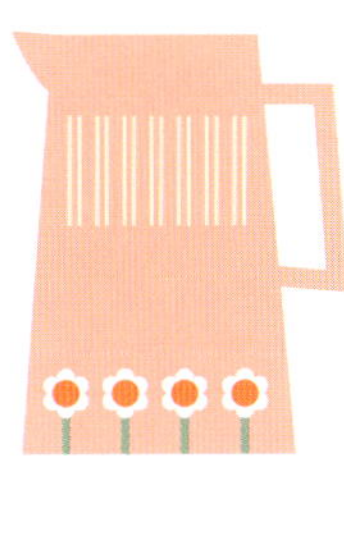

It's easy to be a "good cook" with a PREWAY Trailer Range

that's why they're standard equipment on most trailer coaches.

You'll feel like Mrs. Aladdin when you discover how easy it is to prepare tasty meals on a Preway range. Your fuel is L.P. bottle gas that performs just like gas from city mains, and your range is equipped with all scientific controls so that you can cook, bake or broil with regulated heat.

Even more, compact Preway ranges provide the conveniences you want — an ample working top, uncrowded cooking and baking space, and a durable, porcelain-enamel finish that wipes away clean. All of this is yours with a Preway, plus safe, trouble-free performance regardless of weather or altitude conditions.

For these reasons and many more, most trailer manufacturers equip their coaches with Preway ranges — your clue to a well-designed, good coach home in which cooking can be real fun.

Model P-48731-T
Fully porcelained, all-white front panels, porcelain cooking top, and back rail. Equipped with automatic lighting top burners and Robertshaw oven controls. Large, well-insulated oven and broiler.

Model 4671
Equipped with three large staggered cooking burners, Robertshaw oven controls, hinged grey iron cooking grates, two oven racks, and removable drip tray. Finished in ivory baked enamel.

PRENTISS WABERS PRODUCTS Co.
849 SECOND STREET, N., WISCONSIN RAPIDS, WIS.

Introduction

Traveling has always meant more to me than just seeing new places—it's about discovering the local flavors, hidden gems, and food that tells a story about where you are. In a world where things are starting to look and taste the same everywhere you go, I find myself drawn to the unique—regional dishes, mom-and-pop diners, and recipes that reflect local culture and history.

Before vintage camper trailers took over my life, I owned a little bakery and coffee shop. We roasted our own beans and baked everything from scratch—our muffins and carrot cake were pretty legendary! That love of cooking has always stuck with me. Caroline jokes that I just like to host trailer rallies so I have an excuse to make my pancakes for a crowd, and she's probably right.

This cookbook is a mix of all the things I love: good food, cooking outdoors, and the vintage trailer community that brings it all together. Whether you're whipping something up in a Dutch oven, firing up the grill, or just making sandwiches for the road, I hope you find recipes in this cookbook that you'll come back to again and again. More importantly, I hope they help you create your own great memories around the table—or the picnic bench—wherever your travels take you.

—Paul

HOLD IT!
the NEW
ANDERSON
steals every
The 1952 Anderson Coach is a scene-stealer inside and out!
New exterior styling has resulted in more inside space with only
dimensions.
Inside the new 1952 coaches offer such new features as complete
glass-walled snack bar to separate kitchen from dining area, and til
coordinated interiors make Anderson trailer homes inviting, home-lik
The new 1952 models will continue to incorporate the many "hidden"
Unicoque construction and radiant perimeter heating that have made
favorites with trailerites.
THE 1952 ANDERSON COACH IS AVAILABLE THROUGH AUTHORIZED DEA
• for information write Dept. T.O, Huron Sales Co., East Taw
Anderson Coach Co.

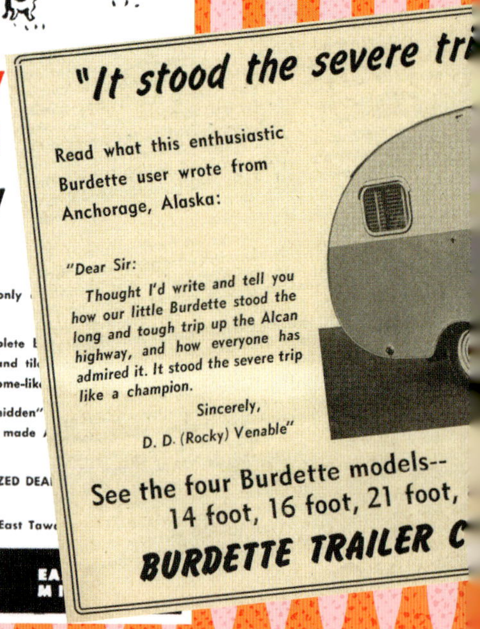
"It stood the severe tr
Read what this enthusiastic Burdette user wrote from Anchorage, Alaska:
"Dear Sir:
Thought I'd write and tell you how our little Burdette stood the long and tough trip up the Alcan highway, and how everyone has admired it. It stood the severe trip like a champion.
Sincerely,
D. D. (Rocky) Venable"
See the four Burdette models--
14 foot, 16 foot, 21 foot,
BURDETTE TRAILER C

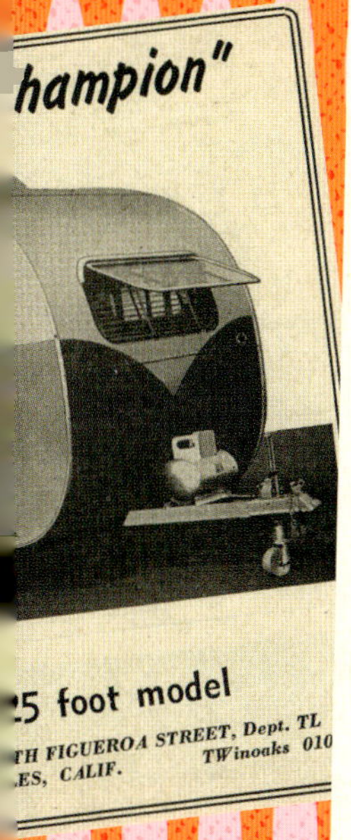

hampion"
25 foot model
TH FIGUEROA STREET, Dept. TL
ES, CALIF. TWinoaks 010

American TRAILER COACHES
HITCH UP AND GO
You'll enjoy new travel freedom with an American Trailer Coach—any place at any time. You take your living accommodations along. You'll have your own wide, restful beds; large, airy living rooms; complete cooking and heating facilities; and insulation for year-'round comfort . . . everything for enjoyable, low-cost traveling or semi-permanent housing. Write for literature on 3 new '48 models.
AMERICAN COACH CO., Cassopolis, Michigan

BREAKFAST

PERFECT PANCAKES

The secret to our pancakes is no secret. It is a "recipe" handed down from my grandmother. We use Krusteaz pancake mix to produce consistent, delicious pancakes every time. When anyone asks, I tell them it's not the recipe, it is how you prepare the mix.

Krusteaz pancake mix
Oil for griddle

1. Follow the instructions on the box. Do not overmix batter! Make the mix on the wet side and be sure to leave some lumps in it.

2. Let the batter sit an hour to an hour and a half before you are ready to make your pancakes to give the batter a chance to "bloom."

3. When you are ready to start cooking, add more water to batter if needed. Blend in the water without overmixing the batter and making sure to leave some of the lumps.

4. Make sure your griddle is very hot! Preheat to 375 degrees F minimum. To check the temperature, drop a little water on your pan or griddle, and if the water dances around the pan, it's ready.

5. Lightly oil the griddle, then wipe the excess off with a paper towel. A little oil goes a long way. You don't want to deep-fry the pancakes.

6. Pour batter onto griddle and cook, a little over a minute on each side. Look for bubbles and dry edges to indicate your pancake is ready to flip.

7. Once you flip the pancake, leave it alone. Do not press down on it or flip it more than once.

8. Serve pancakes two at a time, on a plate, so they are hot and fresh.

- **Tip:** *Use a professional pancake batter dispenser to keep the size of pancakes consistent.*

- **Feeding a Huge Crowd:** *We mix up several 5-gallon buckets of pancake batter. Because we're preparing quantities to serve hundreds of people, we use a paint mixer on a battery-operated drill to blend the water with the mix.*

VARIATIONS

- **Elvis Presley Pancakes:** *Sprinkle cooked and crumbled bacon into each flapjack and serve with peanut butter and bananas.*

- **Strawberry Fields Forever Pancakes:** *Serve with fresh, quartered strawberries tossed with a touch of sugar and topped with whipped cream.*

- **Cinco de Mayo Pancakes:** *Top with Tres Leches Sauce (page 19).*

- **Blueberry Pancakes:** *Gently fold fresh blueberries into the batter.*

- **Kid-Favorite Pancakes:** *Gently fold chocolate chips into the batter.*

OMELET IN A BAG

Making your omelet in a ziplock bag is a fun technique that kids will enjoy. Try one of the combinations below or invent your own!

Ziplock freezer bags
2 to 3 eggs per bag
Ingredients of choice

1. Heat a large pot of water until it reaches a rolling boil.

2. Break the eggs into a resealable bag and toss in your chosen mix-ins. Be sure all meat is fully cooked before adding. If you would like your veggies softer, sauté them before adding as well.

3. Seal the bag securely.

4. Submerge the bag in the boiling water and cook for 12 to 14 minutes.

5. Using caution, as the bag will be hot, remove it from the pot using tongs and carefully open it up.

6. Place your omelet on a plate to serve.

VARIATIONS

- **Classic Denver:** *Ham, onion, green bell pepper, and shredded cheese.*
- **Farmhouse Special:** *Bacon, ham, mushrooms, bell pepper, onion, and shredded Mexican blend cheese.*
- **Fajita Fiesta:** *Seasoned chicken, salsa, onions, bell peppers, and cheese. Serve with a dollop of sour cream and salsa.*

- **Vegetable Garden:** *Bell peppers, onions, mushrooms, and tomatoes. Add your favorite cheese. Try Havarti or Brie.*
- **Carnivore's Delight:** *Bacon, sausage, ham, peppers, onions, and pepper jack cheese.*
- **Sausage and Mushroom:** *Sausage, mushrooms, and Swiss cheese.*
- **Pizza-Style:** *Italian sausage, pepperoni, pizza sauce, and mozzarella. Serve with red pepper flakes and Parmesan.*
- **Spinach and Tomato:** *Fresh spinach, fresh or sun-dried tomatoes, crushed garlic, and feta cheese.*
- **Philly Steak:** *Thin-sliced beef, sautéed onions and peppers, and provolone cheese.*

MAKE-AHEAD BREAKFAST BURRITOS

This hearty breakfast will ensure campers start the day off right.

2 cups breakfast meat (bacon, sausage, or ham)*
1 bag mini Tater Tots
8 eggs
Pinch of salt, cayenne pepper, and fresh ground pepper
2 tablespoons milk
4 burrito-sized flour tortillas
1 cup Mexican blend shredded cheese
Sour cream, guacamole, and salsa for serving

1. Sauté breakfast meat in a skillet and set aside.

2. Cook mini Tater Tots per the instructions and make them extra crispy.

3. In a medium bowl, whisk together eggs, salt, cayenne pepper, pepper, and milk.

4. Cook eggs in a skillet, leaving them slightly underdone.

5. Warm the flour tortillas, place each on a sheet of aluminum foil, and then layer with eggs, cheese, breakfast meat, and Tater Tots.

6. Fold the bottom of each tortilla in toward the filling and roll into a burrito. Wrap in foil, make a flat bottom, and twist the open side of the burrito foil wrapper; this way, you know what side the top is. It is best to wrap burritos with room-temperature fillings.

7. Once cooled, put burritos in a ziplock bag in the freezer.

8. When you pack for camping, put the burritos in a cooler. At camp, heat in a camping oven or put in a skillet to warm

9. Serve with sour cream, guacamole, and salsa.

**Sautéed mushrooms or beans may be substituted.*

Contributed by Carol Mott-Binkley

FLUFFY FRENCH TOAST

A clever way to repurpose leftover hot dog or hamburger buns into golden, fluffy French toast perfect for camping mornings or home brunches. For an alternative twist, turn it into bread pudding with raisins for a hearty dessert (page 154).

4 hot dog or hamburger buns (preferably day-old)
3 large eggs
½ cup milk (or cream for a richer flavor)
1 teaspoon vanilla extract
½ teaspoon ground cinnamon
1 tablespoon sugar
Butter and oil for cooking
Butter, maple syrup, powdered sugar, fruit, and whipped cream for serving

1. Slice the top brown crust off the buns to help the egg mixture absorb better. Split each bun in half or into manageable pieces.

2. In a bowl, whisk eggs, milk, vanilla, cinnamon, and sugar until combined.

3. Dip each piece of bun into the egg mixture, letting it soak for a few seconds.

4. In a skillet or griddle over medium heat, add a little butter and oil. (The butter is good for flavor and the oil keeps the butter from burning.) Cook the soaked buns for several minutes on each side until golden brown.

5. Top with butter, maple syrup, powdered sugar, fresh fruit, and a dollop of whipped cream.

TRES LECHES SAUCE

Drizzle this delicious sauce over pancakes, waffles, or French toast.

2/3 cup sweetened condensed milk
1/2 cup evaporated milk
1/3 cup half-and-half

Combine ingredients in a small saucepan and warm over medium heat. Bring to a boil, stirring constantly for 3 to 4 minutes. Remove from heat and let cool. The consistency will be on the thinner side and very sweet. You can also serve it with cinnamon-sugar and whipped cream.

AUNT JO'S SAUSAGE CHEESE BALLS

These sausage cheese balls are a crowd-pleaser and make for a tasty breakfast.

- 1 pound grated sharp cheddar cheese
- 2 cups baking mix (such as Bisquick)
- 1 pound sausage, cooked and crumbled
- ½ cup water

1. Preheat oven to 350 degrees F.

2. In a large mixing bowl, toss the grated cheese with the baking mix to evenly coat the cheese.

3. Stir in the sausage until well combined.

4. Make a well in the center of the mixture and pour in water. Gently fold the mixture together, being careful not to overmix.

5. Using your hands, shape the mixture into walnut-sized balls (about 1 inch in diameter).

6. Place the balls on a greased or parchment-paper-lined baking sheet. Bake in the preheated oven for 15 minutes, or until golden brown.

7. Allow the sausage cheese balls to cool slightly before serving.

TIPS

- **Refrigerate:** *Store unbaked balls in the refrigerator for up to 24 hours before baking.*
- **Freeze:** *Freeze unbaked balls on a baking sheet until firm, then transfer to a freezer-safe bag. Bake directly from frozen, adding 2 to 3 minutes to the baking time.*

SERVING IDEAS:

Pair with these dips for added flavor:

- *Classic ranch dressing*
- *Honey mustard sauce*
- *Spicy sriracha mayo*
- *Creamy cheese dip*
- *Barbecue sauce*
- *Sweet chili sauce*
- *Hot honey*

Contributed by Thelma Atkinson

NUTRITIOUS FIG GRANOLA BARS

Try these bars as a filling, grab-and-go breakfast or snack.

FIG FILLING

2 cups dried figs, stems removed
1/4 cup water
1 tablespoon lemon juice
1 teaspoon vanilla extract

GRANOLA BAR BASE

1 1/2 cups rolled oats
1/2 cup almond flour (or finely ground almonds)
1/2 cup chopped nuts (walnuts, pecans, or almonds)
1/4 cup unsweetened shredded coconut (optional)
1/4 cup ground flaxseeds or chia seeds
1 teaspoon cinnamon
1/4 teaspoon salt
1/4 cup natural almond butter or peanut butter
1/4 cup honey or maple syrup
2 tablespoons coconut oil, melted
1 teaspoon vanilla extract

1. In a small saucepan, combine the dried figs and water. Simmer over low heat for 5 to 7 minutes, until the figs are soft and the water is mostly absorbed. Transfer to a food processor and blend with the lemon juice and vanilla until smooth. Set aside.

2. Preheat oven to 350 degrees F. Line an 8 x 8-inch baking dish with parchment paper.

3. In a large bowl, mix the rolled oats, almond flour, nuts, coconut, flaxseeds, cinnamon, and salt.

4. In a separate bowl, whisk together the almond butter, honey, coconut oil, and vanilla.

5. Pour the wet ingredients into the dry ingredients and stir until fully combined. The mixture should hold together when pressed.

6. Press half of the granola mixture evenly into the bottom of the prepared baking dish. Spread the fig filling evenly over the granola base. Top with the remaining granola mixture, pressing gently to create an even layer.

7. Bake for 20 to 25 minutes, or until the edges are golden brown. Let cool completely in the pan before slicing.

8. Cut into bars or squares. Store in an airtight container at room temperature for up to 3 days or refrigerate for up to a week. These bars can also be frozen for longer storage.

TIPS FOR CAMPING:

- *Wrap individual bars in parchment paper or aluminum foil for easy grab-and-go servings.*
- *Pair with fresh fruit or yogurt for a balanced camping breakfast.*

TRAILBLAZER'S OVERNIGHT OATS

Overnight oats are a simple, customizable option you can prep at home before you leave on your camping trip. After soaking overnight, these oats become a creamy and delicious breakfast, perfect for a quick start to your outdoor adventure.

OATS

1 part plain old-fashioned oats (not quick oats or steel-cut oats)
1 part milk (you can also use water or plant-based milk)

TOPPINGS

Sweetener (brown sugar or honey)
Fruit
Dried fruit
Nuts
Seeds
Peanut butter
Yogurt

1. Combine ingredients for oats in a container with a portion for one person.

2. Let sit for at least 2 hours or, better, overnight.

3. Top with toppings of your choice.

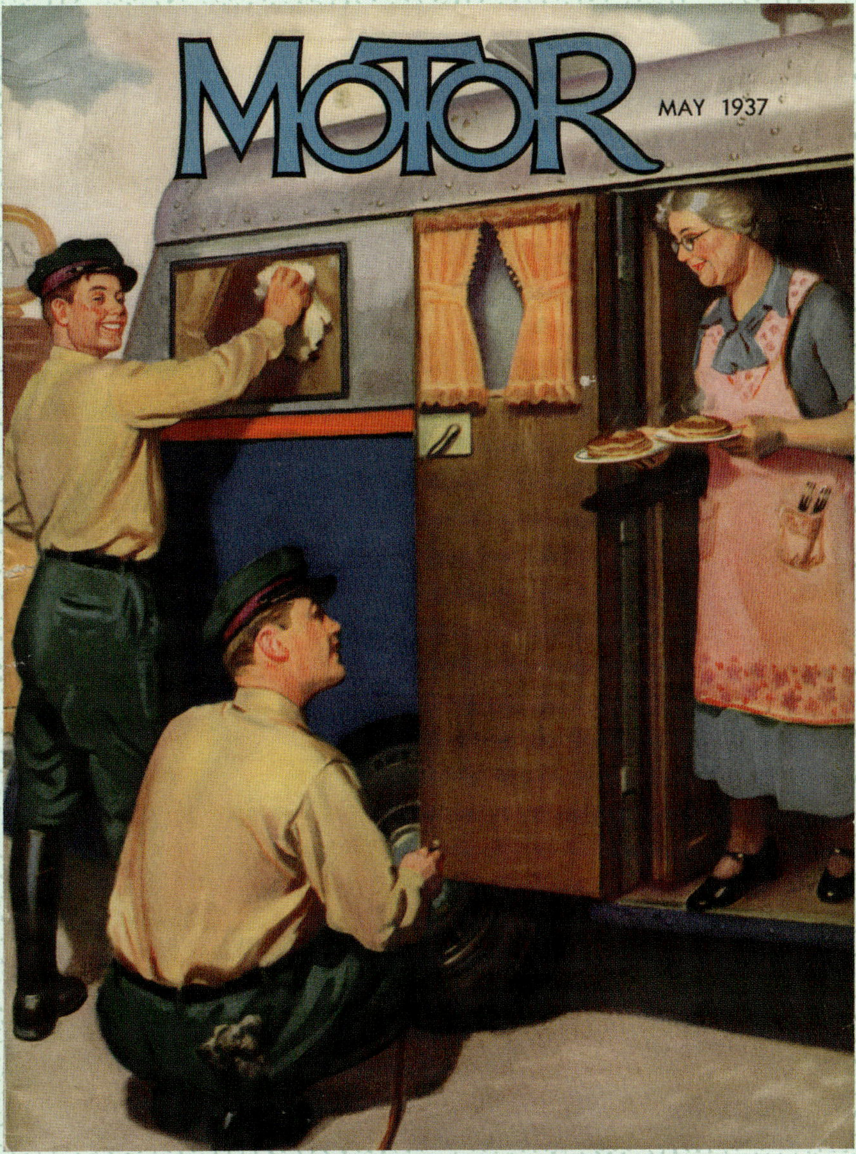
MOTOR
MAY 1937

WHADINGER STICK

A Whadinger stick is a campfire cooking tool made from a long, sturdy stick or dowel and slightly tapered at the end.

1 dowel or stick
Coconut oil or avocado oil

1. **Choose the stick:** Use a dowel or stick that's at least 1 inch in diameter and about 2 to 3 feet long for safe handling near the fire. A closet dowel works well. (You can also attach a 6-8 inch piece of closet dowel to the end of a smaller 3-foot dowel to make it lighter weight.)

2. **Prepare the tip:** Sand the end of the stick so it is smooth and rounded. Slightly tapering your stick makes it easier for wrapping dough.

3. **Season with oil:** When choosing an oil to coat your stick for campfire cooking, you'll want something that can withstand heat and won't go rancid quickly, such as coconut oil or avocado oil. Avoid vegetable oil, olive oil, butter, or lard.

WHADINGER BREAKFAST BISCUITS

Whadinger *is a term often used colloquially, but the origin of the name is somewhat elusive. These campfire treats are widely recognized by other names such as "doughboys," "bannock on a stick," "biscuit cups," or "bread on a stick." Their concept is rooted in traditional methods of cooking bread or dough over an open flame. Native cultures, pioneers, and campers have all used similar methods to create portable, adaptable meals.*

- 1 can of refrigerated biscuit dough (such as Pillsbury)
- Butter or cooking spray for greasing
- Optional fillings (see ideas below)

1. Lightly grease the foil-covered end of your Whadinger stick with butter.

2. Flatten a biscuit slightly with your hands and wrap it around the foil-covered end of the stick. Stretch and pinch the dough to seal the edges, creating a hollow, cuplike shape. Ensure the dough is evenly distributed to avoid burning.

3. Hold the stick over glowing embers (not direct flames) and rotate it slowly to cook the biscuit evenly. This will take 8 to 12 minutes. The biscuit is done when it's golden brown and easily slides off the stick.

4. Let the biscuit cool slightly before filling it with your favorite ingredients.

BREAKFAST WHADINGER FILLINGS

- *Scrambled eggs*
- *Cooked and crumbled sausage*
- *Diced ham*
- *Sautéed sliced mushrooms*
- *Sautéed diced green peppers*
- *Diced tomatoes*
- *Shredded cheese*

MAIN DISHES

MOROCCAN LAMB STEW

If you're looking for something new and different, try this one-pot stew. This pairs beautifully with saffron rice, couscous, pita, or even a hearty rustic bread for a perfect accompaniment to soak up all the delicious flavors. The spices in this recipe mimic ras el hanout, a Moroccan spice blend you can buy online.

1 large yellow onion, chopped
3 carrots, cut into quarter-inch slices
6 small potatoes, peeled and cubed
2 tablespoons olive oil
3 to 5 large garlic cloves, roughly chopped
Salt and pepper
2 to 3 pounds lamb shoulder, cut into large chunks
1 cinnamon stick
1 bay leaf
1½ teaspoons ground allspice
½ teaspoon each ground ginger, cumin, and turmeric
¼ teaspoon cinnamon
¼ teaspoon black pepper
A pinch each white pepper, coriander seed, cayenne, nutmeg, and cloves
1 (15-ounce) can of tomatoes, chopped
2½ cups low-sodium beef broth
1 (15-ounce) can chickpeas

1. In a large Dutch oven over medium heat, sauté the onion, carrots, and potatoes for 5 minutes in olive oil. Add the garlic and season with salt and pepper. Remove the vegetables and set aside.

2. Brown the lamb on all sides in the same pot with olive oil. Season with salt and pepper.

3. Return the sautéed vegetables to the pot along with the cinnamon stick, bay leaf, and all the spices. Stir to coat.

4. Add the tomatoes and broth and bring everything to a boil for 5 minutes.

5. Cover the pot and cook in oven at 350 degrees F for 1 $^{1}/_{2}$ hours. Check occasionally to add water or broth if needed.

6. Add the chickpeas and cook, covered, for another 30 minutes.

BARREL-COOKED TRI-TIP

Using the barrel-cooked method makes a memorable camp cooking experience!

2 tri-tip roasts (2 to 3 pounds each, trimmed of excess fat)
1/4 cup olive oil
2 tablespoons salt
1 tablespoon black pepper
1 tablespoon garlic powder
1 tablespoon smoked paprika
1 teaspoon chili powder (optional)

EQUIPMENT

- **Barrel cooker** *(like a drum smoker or vertical cooker)*
- **Meat hooks** *or grill grate (depending on your setup)*
- **Meat thermometer**
- **Hardwood chunks or wood chips** *(oak is traditional, but hickory or mesquite work well too)*

1. Season the tri-tip by rubbing the roasts generously with olive oil.

2. Mix the dry seasonings in a small bowl and apply evenly across all sides of the roasts.

3. Let the tri-tip sit at room temperature for 30 minutes to absorb the flavors.

4. Light charcoal in the bottom of the barrel. Allow it to ash over before adding your hardwood chunks for smoke.

5. If your barrel has a grill grate, set it in place. Use meat hooks to hang the tri-tips for a more traditional barrel cooking method or place them on the grill grate.

6. Close the lid and let the barrel work its magic. Maintain a consistent medium-low heat, about 275 degrees F.

7. Smoke and cook the tri-tip for about 1 1/2 to 2 hours, depending on its size.

8. Use a meat thermometer to monitor the internal temperature, about 130 to 135 degrees F for medium-rare and 140 to 145 degrees F for medium.

9. Remove the tri-tip from the barrel once it reaches your desired doneness. Wrap in aluminum foil and let it rest for 10 to 15 minutes to redistribute juices.

10. Slice thinly against the grain for maximum tenderness.

TIPS

- **Flavor Profiles:** *For a different spin, marinate the tri-tip overnight in a mix of soy sauce, Worcestershire sauce, and red wine vinegar before seasoning.*
- **Smoky Layers:** *Experiment with different wood chips to change the smoke flavor—applewood adds a sweet note, while pecan is mild and nutty.*
- **Pairing:** *Serve with chimichurri, grilled vegetables, or a hearty potato salad to complement the rich, smoky meat.*

SWEET CHILI SAUSAGES

Sweet chili sausages are a super simple crowd-pleaser and perfect for potlucks. You can heat this up quickly in a pot or set it and forget it in a slow cooker for a couple of hours. The chili sauce isn't spicy, but you can use red pepper flakes to spice it up. Serve over rice.

5 pounds kielbasa
1 (20-ounce) can pineapple chunks, juice reserved
1 (32-ounce) bottle sweet chili sauce
Red pepper flakes (optional)

1. Lightly grill the sausage to give it color and a savory, smoky favor.

2. Cut the sausage into 2-inch pieces.

3. Strain pineapple (reserve liquid for use in Hawaiian Chicken Marinade, page 40).

4. In a slow cooker or pot, combine sausage, pineapple, chili sauce, and red pepper flakes, if using.

5. Heat through and serve.

TROPICAL LUAU FEAST

Tiki is a popular theme for vintage trailer rallies, so dishes inspired by island flavors are a favorite time after time. We serve Island-Style Sweet Chili Sausages and Hawaiian Chicken with loads of white rice made in a commercial 64-cup rice cooker. Add Hawaiian rolls and a green salad or slaw for a complete meal. If serving as a potluck dish, cut the chicken into pieces and serve over rice in a chafing dish.

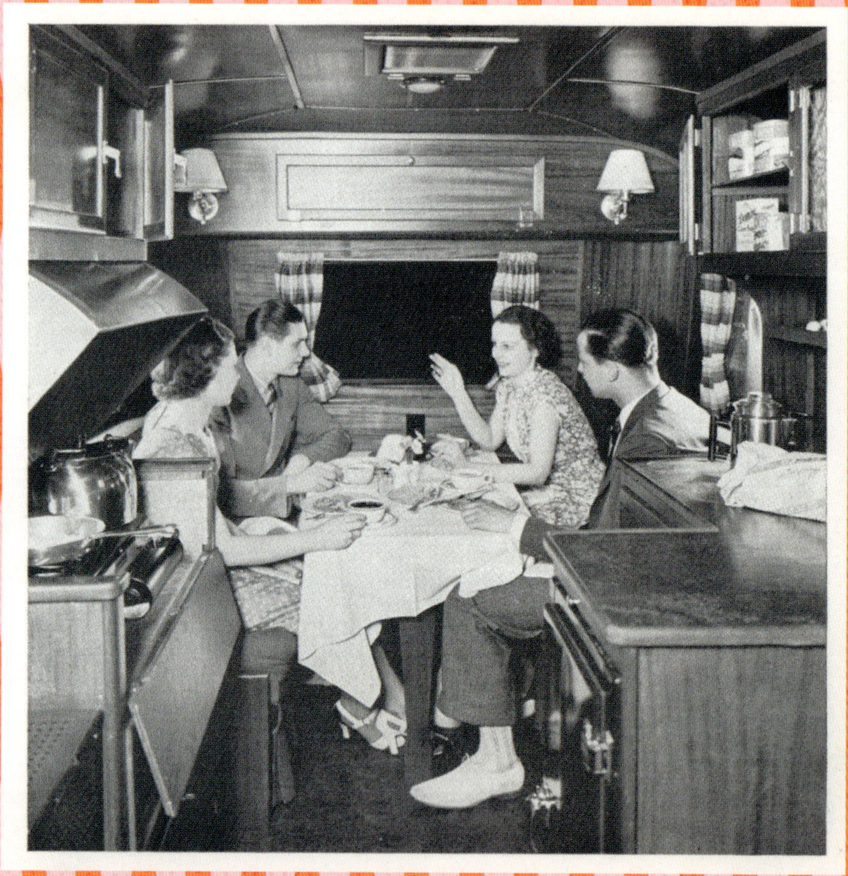

GREEK CHICKEN SKEWERS

The first night at camp can be hectic getting everything set up. You can premake this dish so it marinates while you travel and can be grilled fresh when you arrive at camp. You can also precook it if you just want to heat it up and serve it. We love the flavor combinations.

2 tablespoons olive oil
3 tablespoons lemon juice (1 to 2 lemons)
1 teaspoon paprika
2 teaspoons dried oregano
2 teaspoons dried basil
1 teaspoon dried thyme
3 garlic cloves, minced
1 shallot, diced
Salt and pepper, to taste
2 pounds boneless, skinless chicken thighs, cut into 1-inch pieces

1. In a medium bowl, combine the olive oil, lemon juice, paprika, oregano, basil, thyme, garlic, shallot, and salt and pepper.

2. Coat the chicken in the marinade in a ziplock bag for at least 2 hours or overnight.

3. Thread chicken onto metal or wood skewers. (If using wood skewers, soak in water first for 30 minutes to prevent scorching.)

4. Brush with olive oil; season with more salt and pepper.

5. Preheat the grill to medium heat and cook, turning occasionally, until the chicken is completely cooked through. Chicken should always reach an internal temperature of 165 degrees Fahrenheit. Because the chicken is in chunks, this will only take 10 to 12 minutes.

Serve immediately or let cool and remove from skewers to pack for your trip. Serve this with a fresh green salad with tomatoes and cucumbers. Pack some pita bread and tzatziki to go with the chicken. Long-grain rice also pairs well and makes a nice sit-down meal.

HAWAIIAN CHICKEN

Serve this delicious chicken at your next campout party.

$^1/_2$ cup canned pineapple juice (reserved from Sweet Chili Sausages, page 36)
$^1/_3$ cup olive oil
$^1/_3$ cup packed light brown sugar
$^1/_4$ cup soy sauce
1 teaspoon each ground ginger, onion powder, and garlic powder*
Red pepper flakes (optional)
2 pounds boneless, skinless chicken thighs

1. Combine all the ingredients except chicken together in a large freezer bag. (This can be made in advance to save time at camp.) Reserve $^1/_4$ cup for basting chicken while grilling.

2. Add the chicken to the marinade, seal it without air in the bag, and turn it to coat. Marinate for 4 to 24 hours (max of 12 hours if using chicken breasts rather than thighs).

3. Heat grill to medium-high heat, about 375 to 400 degrees F. Lightly grease the grill and add chicken. Cook for 6 to 8 minutes per side until it is no longer pink and a thermometer registers at 165 to 175 degrees F. Baste the chicken with the reserved marinade for the final few minutes of cooking.

**You can also use fresh garlic and ginger. I use a tablespoon of each.*

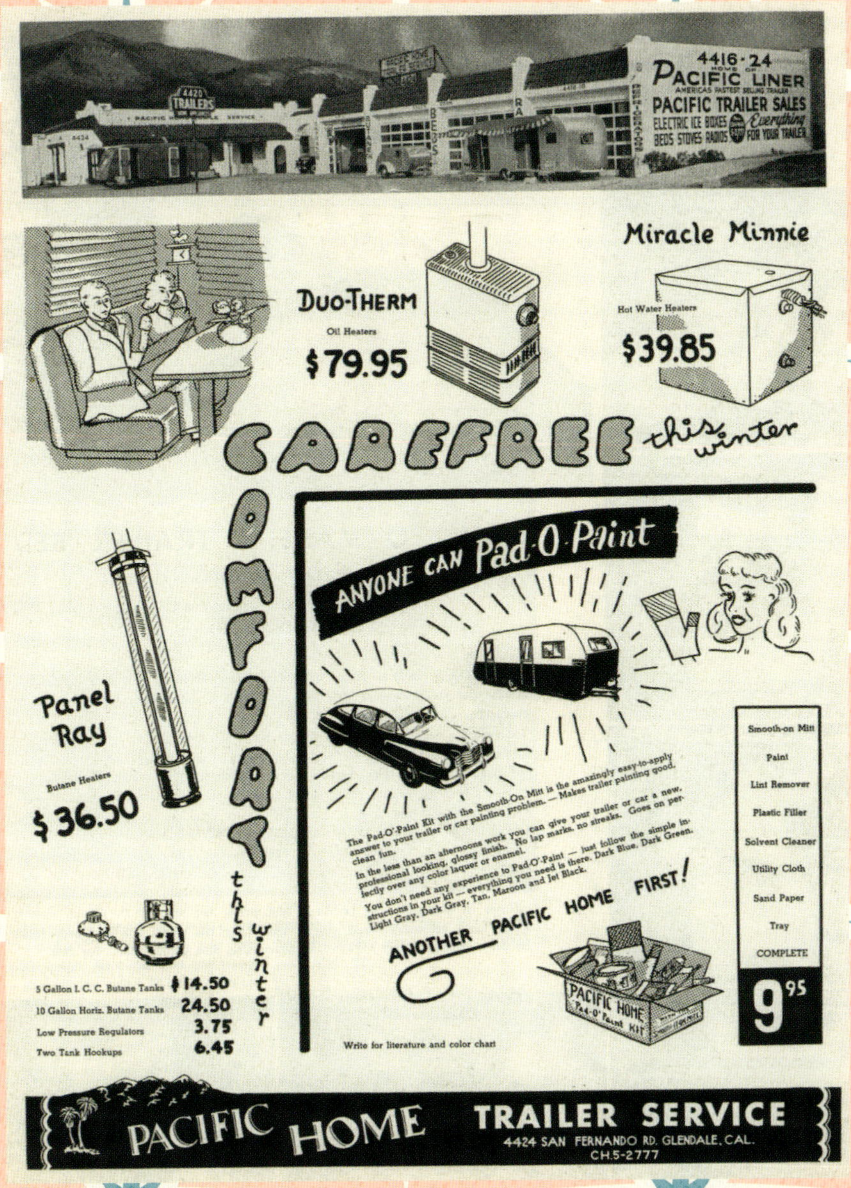

4420
TRAILERS
4424
4416·24
HOME OF
PACIFIC LINER
AMERICAS FASTEST SELLING TRAILER
PACIFIC TRAILER SALES
ELECTRIC ICE BOXES
BEDS STOVES RADIOS
Everything FOR YOUR TRAILER
Duo-Therm
Oil Heaters
$79.95
Miracle Minnie
Hot Water Heaters
$39.85
CAREFREE this winter
COMFORT this winter
Panel Ray
Butane Heaters
$36.50
5 Gallon I. C. C. Butane Tanks $14.50
10 Gallon Horiz. Butane Tanks 24.50
Low Pressure Regulators 3.75
Two Tank Hookups 6.45
ANYONE CAN Pad-O-Paint
The Pad-O'-Paint Kit with the Smooth-On Mitt is the amazingly easy-to-apply answer to your trailer or car painting problem. — Makes trailer painting good, clean fun.
In the less than an afternoons work you can give your trailer or car a new, professional looking, glossy finish. No lap marks, no streaks. Goes on perfectly over any color laquer or enamel.
You don't need any experience to Pad-O'-Paint — just follow the simple instructions in your kit — everything you need is there. Dark Blue, Dark Green, Light Gray, Dark Gray, Tan, Maroon and Jet Black.
ANOTHER PACIFIC HOME FIRST!
PACIFIC HOME Pad-O' Paint KIT
Smooth-on Mitt
Paint
Lint Remover
Plastic Filler
Solvent Cleaner
Utility Cloth
Sand Paper
Tray
COMPLETE
9.95
Write for literature and color chart
PACIFIC HOME TRAILER SERVICE
4424 SAN FERNANDO RD. GLENDALE, CAL.
CH.5-2777

THE PRINCETON

Modern design and precision skill has achieved a noteworthy success in the Princeton—23 feet overall length—a mighty practical, beautiful, and livable trailer coach . . . and definitely a mighty fine buy.

THE PRINCETON LIVING ROOM

▲ VIEW LOOKING THROUGH

↓ BEAUTIFUL, PRACTICAL KITCHEN

THE BEDROOM

CAMPERS' BURRITO BOWL

We often take turns planning dinners with other campers and then get together and share meals. For each "together night," we all bring an ingredient. Here's the no-fuss, one-pot meal to build your own burrito bowl (no tortillas required). And it's quick and easy to clean up afterward because everyone takes their own serving dishes and pans away.

Cooked grilled chicken, seasoned ground beef, beef, pork, or shrimp
Cooked white or brown rice
2 (15-ounce) cans black beans
2 (15-ounce) cans corn
1 (2.25-ounce) can sliced olives
1 (8-ounce) bag shredded Mexican blend cheese
Salsa
Guacamole
Diced onion
Chopped fresh cilantro
Shredded lettuce
Tortilla chips

Set out all ingredients to make a "burrito bar" for individual selection choices.

Contributed by Toni Miltenberger

SPICY ITALIAN CHOPPED SANDWICH

This favorite is full of flavor and very filling. The ingredients can be prepared ahead of time. Toss with dressing and assemble just before you eat while on the road or when you get to the campsite. Consider how many portions you are making and use the amount of ingredients you need. Like most Italian cooking, you can eyeball it and adjust the quantities.

FOR THE SANDWICH

Salami
Pepperoni
Ham
Pepper jack, provolone, or mozzarella cheese
Black olives or other favorites
Artichoke hearts
Tomatoes
Romaine lettuce
Raw or roasted bell pepper (optional)
Red onion (optional)

FOR THE DRESSING

Mayonnaise
Red wine vinegar
Olive oil
Italian seasoning
Red pepper flakes (optional)

1. On a cutting board, chop the sandwich ingredients into small, uniform-sized pieces.

2. In a small bowl, whisk together mayonnaise, vinegar, oil, and Italian seasoning to make the dressing. You can use garlic mayonnaise or add a bit of mustard if you like.

3. Toss the dressing with the chopped sandwich ingredients.

4. Use the mixture to fill rolls for sandwiches or tortillas for wraps and eat right away.

More for your money in the 1949 MAIN-LINE Silver Fleet Trailers
The discriminating eye quickly approves the new 1949 features of Main-Line trailers. All models have the Hollywood door for added light and ventilation, venetian blinds, and bottle-gas for cooking and heating as standard equipment. Oil heaters available in all models.
4 inch double floor in the "Lark" "Lodger" and "Liner"
"Silver-Lodger" 18 ft. Has 16' body, 2 rooms. Features the new "L" kitchen, full size permanent bed. Electric refrigeration available in the Silver-Lodger & Silver-Liner.
"Silver-Lark" 16½ ft. 14' body. Sleeps 4.
"Silver-Liner" 22 ft.... 20' body. 3 rooms Luxury Coach.
More Values than ever before! Compare Main-Line in price and value received; compare weight and tow-ability, with all others, and you'll agree that Main-Line is "America's Greatest Trailer Value"
Silver
Liner
Lodger
Lark
Loafer
ATTENTION DEALERS!
A new factory in Evansville, Indiana will soon serve you.
Write today for free illustrated Silver Fleet folder and the address of the nearest dealer.
MAIN-LINE TRAILER COACH CO., Dept. TL
8825 Avalon Boulevard, Los Angeles 3, California
The Home of the "Silver-Lark"

SMOKY AND TENDER BABY BACK RIBS

Here's a fantastic recipe for slow-cooked ribs done over indirect heat on the grill. This method will infuse the ribs with a smoky flavor while making them incredibly tender, perfect for a summer cookout or camping trip.

FOR THE RIBS

2 racks of baby back ribs
1/4 cup yellow mustard (for coating)

FOR THE DRY RUB

1/4 cup brown sugar
1 tablespoon paprika
1 tablespoon black pepper
1 tablespoon salt
1 tablespoon garlic powder
1 tablespoon onion powder
1 teaspoon chili powder
1 teaspoon smoked paprika
1/2 teaspoon ground cumin
1/2 teaspoon ground mustard
1/4 teaspoon cayenne pepper (optional)

FOR COOKING

1/2 cup apple juice or apple cider vinegar in a spray bottle
1 cup of your favorite barbecue sauce, for finishing glaze (optional)

1. Start by removing the membrane from the back of the ribs. You can do this by gently lifting it with a butter knife and pulling it off with your hands or a paper towel for grip. Pat the ribs dry with paper towels.

2. Rub a thin layer of yellow mustard over both sides of the ribs. This helps the dry rub stick and also enhances the flavor without leaving a mustard taste.

3. Mix all of the dry rub ingredients together in a bowl.

Continued >>

4. Generously coat both sides of the ribs with the dry rub, pressing it into the meat to ensure it adheres well.

5. If using a charcoal grill, set up your grill for indirect heat by placing the coals on one side of the grill. Leave the other side empty to create a hot side and a cooler side for indirect cooking.

6. If using a gas grill, preheat to low, around 225 to 250 degrees F. Turn on only one side of the burners to create indirect heat.

7. Place a small handful of wood chips (such as hickory, applewood, or cherrywood) in a smoker box—or wrap them in foil with holes poked in it—and place directly on the coals or heat source to create smoke.

8. Place the ribs on the grill on the cool side for indirect heat, bone-side down.

9. Close the lid and cook for 2 1/2 to 3 hours, maintaining a grill temperature of 225 to 250 degrees F. Occasionally, spray the ribs with apple juice to keep them moist and help them absorb the smoke flavor.

10. During the last 30 to 40 minutes of cooking, gently pull on a bone to check the ribs for tenderness. The meat should start pulling away from the bone, and the ribs should be tender but not falling apart.

11. In the final 15 to 20 minutes of cooking, brush a generous layer of barbecue sauce over the ribs if using and if you prefer a sticky glaze. Close the lid and allow the sauce to set and caramelize.

12. Once the ribs are done, remove them from the grill and let them rest for about 10 minutes to allow the juices to redistribute.

13. Slice between the bones, serve, and enjoy the smoky, tender goodness.

- **Serving Suggestions:** *Serve your smoky baby back ribs with classic sides like coleslaw, grilled corn on the cob, or fresh potato salad. For an added smoky flavor, consider serving them with a side of grilled vegetables or a baked potato.*

TIPS FOR PERFECT SLOW-COOKED RIBS

- **Keep the lid of the grill closed** *as much as possible to maintain a consistent cooking temperature.*
- **Use a meat thermometer** *to check the internal temperature if you're unsure. The ribs are ready when they reach an internal temperature of around 190 degrees F, but they'll start becoming tender around 180 degrees F.*
- **Rest the ribs** *after cooking to lock in moisture and make them more tender.*

PESTO SKIRT STEAK WAGON WHEELS

These skirt steak roll-ups are a deliciously indulgent combination of juicy steak, savory pesto, and gooey cheese. The dish can be cooked either on the grill for a smoky char or in a cast-iron Dutch oven for a tender, juicy finish. Both methods deliver exceptional flavor.

- 1½ to 2 pounds skirt steak, trimmed
- Salt and pepper to taste
- ½ cup store-bought basil pesto
- 1 cup shredded mozzarella or provolone cheese
- ¼ cup grated Parmesan cheese
- ½ cup sliced roasted red peppers
- ¼ cup sun-dried tomatoes, chopped
- Olive oil for brushing

PREPARE THE STEAK

1. Lay the skirt steak flat on a cutting board. If the steak is thick, butterfly it carefully to create an even layer for rolling. Pound gently with a meat mallet to ensure uniform thickness.

2. Lightly season the steak with salt and pepper on both sides. Spread a thin layer of pesto across the top surface of the steak.

3. Sprinkle shredded mozzarella and Parmesan evenly over the pesto. Layer roasted red peppers and sun-dried tomatoes on top.

4. Roll the steak tightly, starting from the shorter edge. Secure the roll with kitchen twine or toothpicks, spacing them about 1 to 2 inches apart.

Continued →

COOK ON THE GRILL

1. If you are cooking on the grill, preheat to medium-high heat, about 400 degrees F.

2. Brush the roll-ups with olive oil and sear them directly over the heat for 2 to 3 minutes per side to develop a char.

3. Move the roll-ups to indirect heat, close the lid, and cook for an additional 8 to 10 minutes, or until the internal temperature reaches 130 to 135 degrees F for medium-rare.

4. Remove from the grill, tent with foil, and let rest for 5 minutes before slicing.

COOK IN A DUTCH OVEN

1. If you are cooking in a cast-iron Dutch oven, preheat over medium-high heat. Add a drizzle of olive oil.

2. Sear the roll-ups on all sides, about 2 to 3 minutes per side until browned.

3. Reduce heat to low, cover the Dutch oven, and cook for 10 to 15 minutes until the internal temperature reaches 130 to 135 degrees F for medium-rare.

4. Remove the roll-ups from the Dutch oven, cover with foil, and let rest for 5 minutes before slicing.

» **Serving Suggestions:** *Slice the roll-ups into pinwheels and serve warm. Pair with a side of grilled vegetables, garlic mashed potatoes, or a fresh arugula salad with a drizzle of balsamic glaze.*

TIPS

- *For extra flavor, marinate the skirt steak in olive oil, garlic, and Italian seasoning for a few hours before assembling.*
- *Use toothpicks if you don't have kitchen twine but remove them before serving.*
- *Add a sprinkle of crushed red pepper flakes for a slight kick.*

SMOKY BACON CORN SKILLET

This quick and hearty skillet meal combines crispy bacon, tender potatoes, and sweet, creamy corn for a satisfying main dish. Pair with toast or eggs for breakfast or serve with a green salad for lunch or dinner. It's comfort food that's simple to prepare and perfect for busy days or campfire cooking.

1 (12-ounce) package bacon, chopped into 1-inch pieces
2 (15-ounce) cans sliced potatoes, drained
Salt and pepper to taste
2 (14.75-ounce) cans cream-style sweet corn

1. In a large skillet over medium heat, cook the chopped bacon until crispy, stirring occasionally. Once done, use a slotted spoon to remove the bacon to paper towels, leaving the rendered bacon fat in the skillet.

2. Add the sliced potatoes to the skillet with the bacon fat. Cook over medium heat, stirring occasionally, until golden brown and crisp, about 5 to 7 minutes. Season with a pinch of salt and pepper.

3. Reduce the heat to low and stir in the cream-style corn until heated through, about 2 to 3 minutes.

4. Return the crispy bacon to the skillet and mix well. Dish up hot and enjoy!

TIPS

- **Spicy option:** *Sprinkle in a dash of paprika, garlic powder, or crushed red pepper flakes for extra flavor.*
- **Campfire option:** *Cook in a cast-iron skillet over medium-hot coals for a rustic, outdoor-friendly version.*

Submitted by Matt Anderson

New 1949 Zimmer 33-ft., 2-bedroom De Luxe Trailer Home—priced from $3795. Also available as 4-passenger model—priced from $3870.

CAMPFIRE FISH TACOS

This easy and delicious fish taco recipe combines simple ingredients for a fresh, flavorful meal over the campfire. With a creamy mayo slaw, zesty pico de gallo, and perfectly grilled fish, these tacos are sure to please.

FOR THE FISH

1 tablespoon olive oil
1 teaspoon chili powder
1 teaspoon garlic powder
½ teaspoon cumin
Salt and pepper to taste
1 pound whitefish fillets (tilapia, cod, or halibut work well)
8 small soft corn tortillas
Lime wedges for serving

FOR THE MAYO SLAW

1½ cups shredded cabbage (green or a mix of green and purple)
¼ cup mayonnaise
1 tablespoon lemon or lime juice
1 teaspoon mustard
Garlic salt and pepper to taste

FOR THE PICO DE GALLO

2 medium tomatoes, diced
½ red onion, finely diced
1 jalapeño, finely diced (optional)
¼ cup chopped fresh cilantro
Juice of 1 lime
Salt to taste

MAKE THE FISH

1. In a small bowl, mix the olive oil, chili powder, garlic powder, cumin, and salt and pepper.

2. Coat the fish fillets with the seasoning mixture, making sure they're evenly covered.

3. Preheat campfire grill or a heavy skillet over medium heat.

4. Grill the fish for about 3 to 4 minutes per side, or until it is cooked through and flakes easily with a fork.

5. Once done, break the fish into bite-size pieces and set aside.

MAKE THE MAYO SLAW

1. In a bowl, combine the mayonnaise, lemon or lime juice, mustard, and garlic salt and pepper to taste.

2. Add the cabbage and mix to coat.

MAKE THE PICO DE GALLO

1. In a small bowl, mix together the tomatoes, red onion, jalapeño (if using), cilantro, lime juice, and a pinch of salt. Stir well and set aside.

ASSEMBLE THE TACOS

1. Warm the tortillas on your grill or over the campfire until they're soft and slightly charred.

2. Place a few pieces of grilled fish on each tortilla.

3. Top with a spoonful of the mayo slaw and a generous scoop of pico de gallo.

4. Serve the fish tacos hot with lime wedges on the side for extra zest.

TIPS

- *Add a sprinkle of cheese or avocado slices if desired.*
- *If you want a smokier flavor, add a little chipotle powder to the mayo slaw.*

GLAMPER CLAM CHOWDER

A comforting dish to make for a crowd.

- 1/2 pound bacon, diced
- 3 (6.5-ounce) cans of clams, undrained
- 1 yellow onion, diced
- 4 Yukon Gold potatoes, peeled and diced
- 2 stalks celery, diced
- 2 garlic cloves, minced
- 2 cups water
- 1 teaspoon salt
- 1/4 teaspoon coarse-ground black pepper
- 1/2 teaspoon dried thyme
- 2 cups half-and-half
- 2 teaspoons cornstarch
- Sliced green onions, for garnish

1. In a large cast-iron skillet over medium-high heat, cook the bacon until crisp, then remove from the pan. Reserve half for garnish.

2. Add half of the bacon, clams in their liquid, onion, potatoes, celery, garlic, water, salt, pepper, and thyme into the slow cooker and stir.

3. Cook on low for 7 hours.

4. In a measuring cup, whisk together the half-and-half with the cornstarch. Add the half-and-half mixture to the slow cooker and stir.

5. Cook on high for 30 minutes.

6. Serve in bowls garnished with reserved bacon and sliced green onions.

International Balanced 2-Way Heating
(DUCTED plus DIRECTIONAL)

The famous International "Floating Blower", cradled in springs for silent, dependable operation.

Enjoy a "carpet of warmth" throughout your trailer this winter—with a new International Oil Heater. The 2-blower system, exclusive with International, assures *genuine two-way heating.* Luxurious warm air is directed over the floors (where it's needed most) by one blower in the heater base—and a *second* blower, located at the end of the warm air duct, circulates heat to the farthest room.

By drawing the hottest air from the *top* of the heater and using it efficiently in the farthest room, International's "Floating Blowers" *make the warmth go farther—and the fuel last longer!*

Have perfect trailer heating this winter—see your International dealer now.

SPICY SHRIMP AND GRITS

This dish combines smoky, grilled shrimp with creamy, flavorful grits—a perfect camping meal that feels elevated yet easy to prepare.

FOR THE SHRIMP SKEWERS

2 tablespoons olive oil
1 tablespoon smoked paprika
1 teaspoon cayenne pepper
1 teaspoon garlic powder
1 teaspoon onion powder
1/2 teaspoon ground cumin
Salt and black pepper to taste
Juice of 1 lemon, divided
1 pound large shrimp, peeled and deveined (tails optional)

FOR THE GRITS

4 cups water or chicken broth
1 cup quick-cooking grits
1/2 cup shredded sharp cheddar cheese
2 tablespoons butter
1/4 cup heavy cream*
1/2 teaspoon garlic powder
1/2 teaspoon smoked paprika
Salt and pepper to taste

**Whole milk may be substituted*

OPTIONAL GARNISHES

Chopped fresh parsley
Sliced green onions
Hot sauce

PREPARE THE SHRIMP

1. In a resealable bag or container, combine olive oil, smoked paprika, cayenne pepper, garlic powder, onion powder, cumin, salt, pepper, and half the lemon juice.

2. Add shrimp to the bag, seal, and toss to coat. Let marinate for 15 to 30 minutes while you prepare the campfire or other ingredients.

Continued ↣

3. Thread shrimp onto metal or wooden skewers, making sure they're secure but not overcrowded. If you are using wooden skewers, soak in water for 30 minutes ahead of time to prevent charring.

COOK THE GRITS

1. Heat water in a sturdy pot over the campfire or on a camp stove. Bring to a boil.

2. Gradually whisk in the grits to prevent clumping. Lower the heat and cook, stirring often, until thickened (about 5 minutes).

3. Stir in cheese, butter, cream, garlic powder, smoked paprika, and salt and pepper. Adjust seasoning to taste. Cover and set aside to keep warm.

GRILL THE SHRIMP

1. Grill shrimp skewers over medium-high heat on the campfire grate, turning occasionally, until shrimp are pink and slightly charred (about 2 to 3 minutes per side).

2. Remove from the grill and squeeze half of the lemon juice over the top.

ASSEMBLE THE DISH

1. Spoon grits into bowls or plates.

2. Top with grilled shrimp skewers or slide shrimp off skewers onto the grits.

3. Garnish with parsley, green onions, or a drizzle of hot sauce for extra spice.

TIPS

- *Mix shrimp marinade at home to save time.*
- *If you don't have skewers, cook shrimp in a cast-iron skillet over the fire instead.*

CAJUN SHRIMP BOIL

A one-pot dish like a shrimp boil is relatively easy to execute on a propane burner. The potatoes and corn make it economical and filling. In contrast, the shellfish make it a more elevated dish than you may expect when camping.

12 ounces light beer
8 cups water
2 tablespoons Old Bay seasoning, plus more for serving
1 lemon, plus more lemon wedges for serving
1 pound baby red potatoes, washed and cut in half
12 ounces smoked andouille sausage, cut in 2-inch pieces
1 white, yellow, or sweet Vidalia onion, peeled and quartered
4 ears corn, peeled and cut in half
1 pound shrimp, peeled and deveined (tail-on)
¼ cup melted butter, for serving
Louisiana hot sauce, for serving

1. Fill a large pot with beer, water, and Old Bay seasoning. Cut a lemon in half, squeeze the juice of both halves into the pot, and then add the lemon halves to your broth.

2. Bring it all to a boil over high heat. Lower the heat to a healthy simmer.

3. Add the potatoes and cook for about 4 minutes.

4. Add the sausage and onion and cook for another 5 minutes.

5. Add the corn and cook for another 4 to 5 minutes, until corn and potatoes are tender.

6. Add the shrimp and cook for about 2 to 3 minutes. When it is cooked through, it will turn pink.

7. Drain the shrimp boil through a colander (or scoop it out with a large strainer) and transfer to a large platter. It can also be dumped on the table on natural brown butcher paper.

8. Serve with melted butter, lemon wedges, extra Old Bay seasoning in a shaker, and Louisiana hot sauce.

Tip: *The recipe isn't so technical that you have to be exact. Keep the proportions fairly similar, and you can't go wrong.*

KOREAN SALAD BOWL

This salad bowl is like a rice bowl, but with greens or a combination of rice and greens. You can prepare the beef and rice in advance and then package the other ingredients separately in ziplock bags, so it's just a matter of assembling dinner when you get to the campground. This one-dish meal offers several options to customize each bowl.

SALAD

1 pound lean ground beef
3 to 4 garlic cloves, minced
1/4 cup packed brown sugar
1/4 cup reduced-sodium soy sauce
2 teaspoons sesame oil
1/4 teaspoon ground ginger
1/4 teaspoon crushed red pepper flakes
1/4 teaspoon pepper
Salad greens such as romaine lettuce, mixed spring greens, iceberg lettuce, or spinach
2 cups white or brown rice, cooked

TOPPINGS

Grated carrots
Bean sprouts
Edamame
Hearts of palm
Crispy onions
Pickled daikon
Sliced green onions, for garnish
Sesame seeds, for garnish

1. In a skillet, cook the ground beef and garlic over medium heat. Drain the grease.

2. Mix brown sugar, soy sauce, sesame oil, ginger, red pepper flakes, and pepper in a bowl.

3. Add the liquid mixture to the cooked ground beef and let simmer for 2 to 3 minutes. Remove from heat and let cool.

4. Prepare your preferred toppings for assembly when you are ready to serve.

5. Serve with Lao Gan Ma Spicy Chili Crisp, sriracha, sriracha mayo, or ranch dressing.

THE HANSON LOVE BUG TRAILER
• Sold Factory Direct to You
at the Lowest Possible Prices...
the CUSTOMER IS KING
WORLDS LOWEST PRICES
SMALL DOWN PAYMENT •• 5 YEARS TO PAY
HANSON TRAILER SALES
HANSON
TRAILER
SALES

SIMPLE BANH MI

A traditional Banh Mi is a Vietnamese sandwich that combines French influences with bold Asian flavors. While BBQ pork is delicious, you don't need fancy ingredients to enjoy the signature flavors of this beloved dish. With simple, affordable deli meats, you can re-create a budget-friendly version that's just as satisfying and packed with flavor.

FOR THE PICKLED VEGGIES

¼ cup white vinegar
¼ cup water
1 tablespoon sugar
½ teaspoon salt
1 small carrot, julienned
½ daikon radish,* julienned

FOR THE SANDWICH

1 baguette or soft French roll, split lengthwise
1 to 2 tablespoons mayonnaise**
4 to 6 slices of bologna or cotto salami
1 small cucumber, thinly sliced lengthwise
1 to 2 small jalapeños, thinly sliced (optional)
Fresh cilantro sprigs

MAKE THE PICKLED VEGGIES

1. In a small bowl or jar, combine vinegar, water, sugar, and salt. Stir until dissolved.

2. Add carrot and radish to the pickling liquid. Let sit for at least 15 minutes, or longer for a stronger flavor. Drain before using.

ASSEMBLE THE SANDWICH

1. Split the baguette and lightly toast it over a grill, in a skillet, or under a broiler.

2. Spread mayonnaise generously on each piece of bread.

3. Lay the slices of bologna or salami inside the bread.

4. Layer with cucumber, jalapeño (if using), cilantro, and pickled vegetables.

*Regular radish may be substituted.

**Mix mayo with a splash of Sriracha for extra kick.

TIPS

- **Prepare ahead:** *Make the pickled veggies at home and store them in a small jar.*
- **Grilled option:** *Heat the bologna or salami on a campfire grill or skillet for a smoky flavor.*
- **Baguette substitute:** *Use hot dog buns for an ultra-budget-friendly version.*

SOUTHWEST FIESTA SALAD

A colorful, flavorful mix of black beans, corn, peppers, cotija cheese, and creamy avocado, with an optional touch of tropical fruit for sweetness if you like. It's an ideal make-ahead dish for camping. Add the avocado just before serving.

FOR THE SALAD

1 (15-ounce) can black beans, drained and rinsed
1 (15-ounce) can corn, drained*
1 red bell pepper, seeded and diced
½ cup chopped fresh cilantro
1 jalapeño pepper, seeded and diced
⅓ cup diced red onion
¼ cup cotija cheese

FOR THE DRESSING

Juice of 2 to 3 limes
3 tablespoons avocado oil
1 small garlic clove, grated
Salt and pepper

OPTIONAL

1 ripe but firm avocado, diced
Sliced radish or jicama
Fresh mango or pineapple chunks

1. Combine the salad ingredients.

2. In a small bowl, combine lime juice, avocado oil, and garlic. Add salt and pepper to taste.

3. Toss salad ingredients with dressing and serve.

4. This salad keeps refrigerated for several days.

**You can substitute fresh grilled corn cut off the cob.*

The kitchen will delight all women. Your 'galley' is all on one side, with surprising cupboard space and large icebox — eye-level windows — luxury, home environment, wherever you go!

CAMPFIRE BAKED ZITI

When you're camping with your vintage trailer, chilling in the backyard, or hosting friends, this baked ziti recipe is a crowd-pleasing comfort dish. It's simple, adaptable, and made for sharing.

1 pound bulk Italian mild sausage
1 cup diced green bell pepper
1 medium onion, diced
1 cup sliced mushrooms
1 pound ziti pasta, cooked al dente
1 (24-ounce) jar of your favorite spaghetti sauce
2 cups cubed or shredded mozzarella cheese, plus extra for topping

1. Heat a Dutch oven over a bed of coals or stovetop burner.

2. In the Dutch oven, brown the sausage until fully cooked, breaking it up into crumbles as it cooks.

3. Add the green pepper and onion. Cook for 3 to 4 minutes, stirring occasionally, until the vegetables are crisp-tender.

4. Add the mushrooms and cook for another 2 minutes.

5. Stir in the cooked pasta and spaghetti sauce. Mix well to coat everything evenly.

6. Fold in mozzarella cheese, letting it melt slightly as you stir.

7. Cover the Dutch oven with its lid and arrange 16 hot coals on top and 8 underneath. Bake for about 30 minutes until the dish is bubbly and heated through.

8. Sprinkle extra shredded mozzarella on top, cover, and let it melt for a few minutes.

9. Dish it up hot, straight from the Dutch oven. Pair with crusty bread or a fresh side salad for a hearty meal.

VARIATIONS

- *Add diced zucchini, black olives, or spinach.*
- *Replace mild sausage with hot Italian sausage or use ground beef or turkey.*
- *Try ricotta or Parmesan in place of mozzarella.*

AUG 1960

ANGELO'S TRADITIONAL CARBONARA

Our kids are great cooks, each with their own culinary passions. Our Italian food enthusiast Angelo has perfected his go-to dish: spaghetti carbonara. This classic pasta is so luxuriously creamy that you might think it's loaded with cream. But Angelo doesn't take any shortcuts. He prepares it traditionally, just as it was meant to be made. No cream in sight—only eggs, cheese, and a bit of starchy pasta water, coming together in perfect harmony.

8 ounces of pork belly*
Salt and pepper
Garlic powder
Olive oil
Spaghetti, enough for 2 servings
2 egg yolks
1 egg
1 cup fresh grated Parmesan cheese
2 teaspoons minced garlic
3/4 cups frozen peas
2 teaspoons fresh-cracked pepper

1. Dice the pork belly into elongated batons smaller than bite-size. Toss with salt, pepper, and garlic powder, and drizzle with olive oil.

2. Bring salted water to a full boil, add pasta, and cook as directed.

3. Sear the pork belly in a cast-iron skillet with a drizzle of olive oil, rendering the fat.

4. While the pasta and pork are cooking, combine egg yolks, egg, and enough of the grated Parmesan to make a paste.

5. Add garlic to the pork belly in the pan as the pasta gets close to being cooked.

6. Once cooked, drain the pasta gently, reserving 1/4 cup of the pasta water.

7. Add the pasta and reserved cooking liquid to the pork belly mixture and let cool with the heat off for 2 minutes while tossing together.

8. Fold in the frozen peas to cool the mixture further.

9. Finally, add the egg-and-cheese mixture, flipping and stirring continuously until the eggs have become a sauce coating the pasta.

10. Finish with fresh-cracked black pepper and top with remaining grated Parmesan.

***** *You can substitute pancetta or bacon for the pork belly but choose block bacon so you can cut it into chunky batons. Lean bacon won't give you enough fat, so the sauce won't thicken properly.*

Contributed by Angelo Lacitinola

FAMILY FAVORITES

BARBACOA BEEF TACOS

Serve these delicious tacos with any or all of the following: flour or corn tortillas, tortilla chips, rice, pico de gallo, shredded cheese, sour cream, guacamole, cilantro, avocado, and fresh lime wedges.

1 (3-pound) beef chuck roast
Salt and pepper, to taste
Splash of oil
4 chipotle peppers in adobo sauce, chopped
5 garlic cloves, chopped
1 tablespoon ground cumin
3 teaspoons dried oregano
¼ teaspoon ground cloves
½ cup beef broth
¼ cup apple cider vinegar
¼ cup fresh lime juice
3 bay leaves

1. Cut the beef into large chunks. Season with salt and pepper.

2. Heat the oil in a large skillet over medium-high heat. Sear the beef on all sides, until browned, then transfer to a slow cooker (Do this in small batches to keep the heat high enough. You want to sear the meat rather than steaming it.)

3. In a medium bowl, combine the chipotles, garlic, cumin, oregano, cloves, beef broth, apple cider vinegar, and lime juice.

4. Pour the mixture over the beef in the slow cooker and add the bay leaves. Cover and cook on low for 8 hours or until the meat can be shredded easily.

5. Remove the bay leaves. Shred the beef with two forks to serve.

CHILI CON CARNE

Chili con carne is more than just a hearty meal; it's a dish steeped in rich tradition and bold flavors. Originating from the southwestern United States, this spicy stew made of meat, chili peppers, and savory spices has become a beloved comfort food across the country and beyond. Whether served at a backyard cookout, shared around a campfire, or enjoyed on a cold night, chili con carne brings warmth and satisfaction with every bite.

3 pounds ground beef
1 medium onion, diced
1 large green bell pepper, diced
4 garlic cloves, finely chopped or crushed
1 (28-ounce) can tomato sauce
1 (28-ounce) can diced tomatoes
1 (10.75-ounce) can tomato soup
2 (14-ounce) cans beans in tomato sauce
1 (15-ounce) can kidney beans, drained
2 tablespoons chili powder
1 tablespoon dried oregano
1/2 tablespoon dried basil
Salt and pepper to taste
Red pepper flakes to taste (optional)

1. In a skillet, brown ground beef on medium-high. Drain the excess fat.

2. Add the onion, bell pepper, and garlic and continue cooking, stirring often, for 5 minutes until the beef is no longer pink. Add to slow cooker.

3. Add all the canned ingredients plus chili powder, oregano, basil, and salt and pepper. Stir to combine.

4. Cook on high for 3 to 4 hours or on low for 6 to 7 hours. Taste and adjust seasonings. Add red pepper flakes if desired for a bit of kick.

GARNISHES

- Sour cream
- Grated cheese
- Pickled or fresh jalapeños
- Sliced green onions
- Finely diced white onion

7-CAN CAMPERS' SOUP

The name of this recipe gives a hint of the ingredients list. Still, it is shy about revealing the actual taste, a cross between tortilla soup and chicken chili. The directions are devastatingly simple, and the hearty, filling dish comes together in 30 minutes. It's the ideal thing to whip up after work. You can even add another can of different beans, making this an 8-can soup!

- 1 (15-ounce) can black beans, drained and rinsed
- 1 (15-ounce) can pinto beans, drained and rinsed
- 1 (14.5 ounce) can diced petite tomatoes
- 1 (15-ounce) can sweet or fire-roasted corn, drained
- 1 (12.5 ounce) can chicken breast, drained and flaked*
- 1 (28-ounce) can green enchilada sauce
- 1 (14-ounce) can low-sodium chicken broth
- 1 (1-ounce) packet taco seasoning
- 1/2 teaspoon cumin
- 1/2 teaspoon chili powder
- 1/2 teaspoon garlic powder
- Shredded cheese, for serving
- Tortillas or corn chips, for serving
- Lime wedges, for serving

1. In a large pot on the stovetop, combine all the canned ingredients and the taco seasoning, cumin, chili powder, and garlic powder.

2. Bring the soup to a boil over medium-high heat.

3. Reduce the heat and let simmer for 20 to 25 minutes.

4. Serve warm with shredded cheese, tortillas, and lime wedges.

*Add a second can for more protein.

Contributed by Debra Smith

DUTCH OVEN BARBECUE CHICKEN

To make this classic dish, use approximately 9 coals on the bottom and 18 coals on the top of a 12-inch cast-iron Dutch oven to bring the temperature to 375 degrees F. Keep in mind that you may need to add more coals or replenish them as they burn out.

1 onion, peeled and sliced
2 tablespoons butter
2 (28-ounce) bottles barbecue sauce
1 cup water
1 whole chicken (or pieces of choice)

1. Brown onion in butter in a Dutch oven over coals.
2. Add the barbecue sauce and water and bring to a simmer.
3. Add the chicken and return to a simmer.
4. Cover and cook for approximately 1 hour.

Contributed by Darline Braun

WAGON MASTER DAVID'S SHEPHERD'S PIE

This family favorite heats up well as leftovers too.

6 medium potatoes, peeled
1 pound extra-lean ground beef or meat of your choice
Favorite seasoning mix or salt and pepper
2 carrots, grated
1 (15-ounce) can peas, drained
1 yellow or white onion, grated
2 tablespoons tomato paste
½ cup beef broth
2 tablespoons red wine
1 tablespoon Worcestershire sauce
1 tablespoon minced garlic
1 cup canned corn, drained
2 egg yolks
⅓ cup heavy whipping cream
2 teaspoons garlic powder
1 cup shredded Parmesan cheese, plus more for topping

1. Get your coals going. When they are ready, put the Dutch oven on top of the coals to warm it up (never put this recipe in a cold Dutch oven).

2. Cut the potatoes in even chunks and add to a large pot. Cover with water and bring to a boil; boil until tender. Drain well.

3. Meanwhile, brown the meat in a cast-iron skillet over medium-high heat. Season with your favorite dry seasoning mix or salt and pepper. Cook until all of the moisture evaporates; drain excess grease if needed.

4. Reduce the heat to medium and stir in the carrots, peas, and onion. Stir in the tomato paste and beef broth, until smooth. Cook about 5 minutes, stirring occasionally.

5. Stir in the wine, Worcestershire sauce, garlic, and corn. Cook a few minutes until the dish has warmed through. Set aside.

6. Mash and blend the potatoes until smooth. Beat in the egg yolks, cream, and garlic powder. Beat in the Parmesan cheese.

7. Transfer the meat mixture to a 10-inch Dutch oven and spread evenly. Spoon the finished mashed potatoes on top and use a spatula to spread evenly and to make little whippy peaks.

8. Sprinkle more Parmesan cheese on top of the potatoes.

9. Put the lid on the Dutch oven and cook at 400 degrees F for 30 minutes. Open the lid at 15 minutes to ensure all is cooking properly. Replace the lid and give it a half turn to ensure everything is cooking evenly. The shepherd's pie is done when the top is slightly browned and the whippy peaks are a little more browned than that.

10. Let the dish sit about 5 minutes off the coals with the lid on. After 5 minutes, take the top off and dish it up to your hungry campers.

Contributed by David Neel

CAMPING TIPS

A propane stove on a picnic table works well for boiling the potatoes and browning the ground beef.

A battery-powered drill with a beater from the mixer at home works well for whipping the potatoes.

CAST-IRON FAJITA NACHOS

A perfect marriage of fajitas and nachos, this cast-iron skillet recipe is quick, versatile, and packed with flavor. Use your favorite leftover proteins—steak, pork, chicken, or even a mix—to create a satisfying dish ideal for any camping adventure.

1 tablespoon olive oil
1 small onion, thinly sliced
1 small bell pepper (red, yellow, or green), thinly sliced
2 cups cooked and shredded or diced meat (steak, pork, chicken, or a blend)
1 teaspoon fajita seasoning (store-bought or homemade)
1 bag tortilla chips
1½ cups shredded Mexican blend cheese
½ cup black beans (optional)
½ cup fresh salsa or pico de gallo
¼ cup sliced jalapeños (fresh or pickled)
¼ cup sour cream
2 tablespoons chopped cilantro
1 lime, cut into wedges

1. Heat a cast-iron skillet over the campfire until hot. Add olive oil and sauté the onion and bell pepper until softened and slightly charred, about 5 to 7 minutes.

2. Stir in the cooked protein and fajita seasoning, cooking for 2 to 3 minutes to heat through and coat everything in the seasoning. Remove the mixture from the skillet and set aside.

3. Layer half of the tortilla chips in the skillet. Sprinkle with half of the cheese, black beans (if using), and the fajita mixture. Add a second layer of chips and repeat with the remaining cheese and fajita mixture.

4. Cover the skillet with aluminum foil or a lid and place it over medium heat on the campfire. Let cook for 5 to 7 minutes or until the cheese is melted and bubbly.

5. Remove from the heat and top with salsa or pico de gallo, jalapeños, sour cream, and cilantro. Serve directly from the skillet with lime wedges on the side.

➣ **Extra Toppings:** *Try adding guacamole or hot sauce.*

CAMPFIRE BACON-WRAPPED GOURMET HOT DOGS

This elevated twist on a classic hot dog combines smoky bacon, melted cheese, and flavorful toppings, all cooked over a campfire. It's a crowd-pleaser that's easy to prepare.

6 high-quality hot dogs or sausages (such as bratwurst or smoked sausages)
6 slices thick-cut bacon
Toothpicks or small skewers
6 hot dog buns
1 cup shredded cheese (cheddar, pepper jack, or smoked Gouda)
1/2 cup diced onions
1/2 cup diced jalapeños (optional)
1/4 cup barbecue sauce or honey mustard for drizzling (optional)

1. Wrap each hot dog tightly with a slice of bacon, securing the ends with toothpicks.

2. Place the bacon-wrapped hot dogs on a grill grate or use a campfire skewer. Cook over the fire, turning frequently, until the bacon is crispy and fully cooked, about 8 to 10 minutes.

3. Place the buns on the grill grate for 1 to 2 minutes to lightly toast, if desired.

4. Put the cooked hot dogs in the buns. Top with shredded cheese, diced onions, and jalapeños if desired. For extra flavor, drizzle with barbecue sauce.

5. Wrap each assembled hot dog in aluminum foil and place near the fire for 1 to 2 minutes to melt the cheese.

6. Carefully remove the foil and toothpicks and serve immediately. Enjoy your gourmet campfire hot dogs!

VARIATIONS

- **Mediterranean Style:** *Use lamb sausages and top with feta, diced cucumbers, and tzatziki sauce.*
- **Classic Reuben:** *Swap the bacon for pastrami and top with Swiss cheese, sauerkraut, and Thousand Island dressing.*
- **Tex-Mex:** *Add guacamole, salsa, and Mexican blend cheese.*

GRANDMA MANDY'S GRILLED CHEESE WITH JELLY POCKETS

This delightful sandwich combines the gooey goodness of melted cheese with the sweet surprise of jelly, all toasted to perfection in a pie iron. Grandma Mandy Brandt's recipe is a cherished family treat that brings back childhood memories.

- 1 to 2 tablespoons butter, softened
- 2 slices sandwich bread (good old white bread will work)
- 1 slice of your favorite cheese (American, cheddar, or provolone work well)
- 1 to 2 tablespoons fruit jelly or jam (grape, strawberry, or your favorite flavor)

1. Spread butter on one side of each bread slice. The buttered sides will be the outside of the sandwich for toasting.

2. Place one slice of bread, butter-side down, into one half of the pie iron.

3. Add the slice of cheese on top of the bread, ensuring it fits inside the edges.

4. Spoon the jelly onto the center of the cheese, spreading slightly but leaving space around the edges to avoid leaks.

5. Top with the second slice of bread, butter-side up.

6. To cook the sandwich, close the pie iron, pressing gently to seal the edges. Trim any excess bread if needed.

7. Hold the pie iron over the campfire, hot coals, or a grill. Cook for about 3 to 4 minutes on each side, checking periodically to ensure it doesn't burn. The sandwich is ready when the bread is golden brown and crispy and the cheese is melted.

TIPS FOR SUCCESS

- **Cool slightly before eating:** *Let the sandwich cool a little before enjoying it—watch out for hot jelly!*
- **Avoid overfilling:** *Too much jelly can leak out and make a mess in the pie iron.*
- **Customize:** *Try different cheese and jelly combinations—Brie with raspberry jam is a decadent twist.*

WHAT IS A PIE IRON?

A pie iron is a cast iron or aluminum cooking tool with two hinged plates that clamp together to hold bread or dough and fillings. Creating sealed "pockets" of deliciousness, it's perfect for everything from savory sandwiches to sweet desserts. The pie iron is versatile and easy to use—it's ideal for campfire cooking.

WARDROBE
ICE BOX
WARDROBE
HEAT
WARDROBE
Member Trailer Coach Manufacturers Association
ELCAR COACH
PRODUCT OF ELCAR COACH CORPORATION
831 South Wabash Ave., Chicago 5, Illinois

NEXT-LEVEL GRILLED CHEESE SANDWICH

Elevate the classic grilled cheese with unique twists, bold flavors, and a combination of textures that will make each bite irresistible. The base of sourdough bread and creamy Havarti cheese is just the beginning.

2 tablespoons unsalted butter,* softened
2 slices thick-cut sourdough bread
2 slices Havarti cheese

1. Spread a thin layer of softened butter on one side of each slice of bread.

2. Place Havarti cheese between the sourdough slices.

3. Heat a cast-iron skillet or heavy pan over medium heat. Once the pan is hot, place the sandwich in the pan, buttered side down. Grill for 3 to 4 minutes on one side until golden brown and crispy.

4. Flip the sandwich carefully and grill the other side for another 3 to 4 minutes, pressing gently to ensure even cooking. Adjust heat if necessary to prevent burning.

5. After the second side is golden and the cheese is melted, remove the sandwich from the pan. Let it rest for a minute before slicing.

Substitute mayonnaise for the butter for an amazing golden crust!

Continued →

VARIATIONS

These variations transform your grilled cheese into something even more indulgent. Add one or more of the following before grilling to create a truly unique and mouthwatering version.

- **Bacon Jam:** *1 tablespoon Bacon Jam (page 144)*
- **Truffle and Parmesan:** *1 teaspoon truffle oil, 1 tablespoon freshly grated Parmesan, a couple grinds of freshly cracked black pepper*
- **Bacon and Caramelized Onion:** *2 to 3 slices crispy bacon, 1⁄4 cup caramelized onions, pinch of thyme or rosemary*
- **Tomato Basil Pesto:** *2 slices ripe heirloom tomato, 1 tablespoon basil pesto, a handful of fresh basil leaves*
- **Spicy Jalapeño and Avocado:** *Sliced jalapeños (fresh or pickled), 1⁄4 avocado (mashed), a drizzle of Sriracha or your favorite hot sauce*
- **Apple and Prosciutto:** *Thinly sliced apple (such as Fuji or Granny Smith), 1 to 2 slices prosciutto, a drizzle of honey or balsamic glaze*
- **BBQ Pulled Pork and Pickles:** *Spoonful BBQ pulled pork, pickle slices (dill or bread-and-butter), sprinkle of smoked paprika*

TIPS

- **Go Low and Slow:** *Don't rush the grilling process. Cooking on medium-low heat allows the cheese to melt perfectly without burning the bread.*
- **Use a Panini Press:** *For an even crispier crust and perfectly melted cheese, use a panini press.*
- **Add Cheese Layers:** *For extra melty goodness, try layering cheeses (Havarti with mozzarella, cheddar, or Gruyère) to create a rich and gooey center.*

THE GALLEY

This spacious and fluorescent lighted galley has been thoughtfully designed to minimize work. It is a woman's dream! The satin finish stainless steel work table top and sink are only part of its beauty. China red waterproof tilac with gleaming white scored lines, edged with aluminum trim moulding is set off by chrome accessories. The ivory ceiling and cabiners add a glowing richness of color. Concealed in the cabinet is an adequate emergency reserve water supply and hookup for running water.

PIZZA FLATBREADS WITH FLAIR

These pizza flatbreads are a fun, creative twist on traditional pizza, perfect for satisfying that pizza craving while camping in an RV. Using premade flatbreads (or naan) as the base, you can quickly assemble personal-sized pizzas and cook them over the campfire or in an RV oven. Or each person can build their own pizza with toppings they love. The result? Crispy, cheesy, and absolutely delicious.

4 flatbreads or naan (store-bought or homemade if you're feeling adventurous)
1 tablespoon olive oil, for brushing
1 cup pizza sauce (store-bought or homemade)
2 cups shredded mozzarella cheese (or a mix of mozzarella and cheddar)
Toppings of your choice
Crushed red pepper flakes (optional)
Fresh basil for garnish (optional)
Salt and pepper to taste

RV OVEN COOKING

1. Preheat the oven to 375 degrees F.

2. Lay out the flatbreads on a clean surface. Brush each one lightly with olive oil on both sides. This will help them crisp up nicely while cooking. Spread a thin layer of pizza sauce over each flatbread, leaving a small border around the edges for the crust.

3. Sprinkle a generous layer of shredded mozzarella (or your preferred cheese) over the sauce. Add your choice of toppings. Be creative and use what you have on hand!

Continued →

4. Place the pizza on a baking sheet or directly on the oven rack. Bake for 10 to 12 minutes until the cheese is melted and the edges are golden brown.

5. To serve, add a sprinkle of fresh basil, Parmesan cheese, crushed red pepper flakes, or a drizzle of olive oil or hot honey for added flavor.

CAMPFIRE COOKING

1. Prepare your coals for indirect heat. A campfire grill grate or cast-iron skillet works great for this.

2. Lay out the flatbreads on a clean surface. Brush each one lightly with olive oil on both sides. This will help them crisp up nicely while cooking. Spread a thin layer of pizza sauce over each flatbread, leaving a small border around the edges for the crust.

3. Sprinkle a generous layer of shredded mozzarella (or your preferred cheese) over the sauce. Add your choice of toppings. Be creative and use what you have on hand!

4. Place the flatbread pizza on a campfire grill grate or cast-iron skillet, covering with a lid or foil. Cook for 5 to 7 minutes, occasionally checking to ensure the crust doesn't burn. If you want a crispier bottom, place the pizza directly on the grill grate over indirect heat for a couple of minutes.

5. To serve, add a sprinkle of fresh basil, Parmesan cheese, crushed red pepper flakes, or a drizzle of olive oil or hot honey for added flavor.

TOPPINGS

- **Keep It Simple:** *Cheese and pizza sauce*
- **Classic Margherita:** *Fresh basil leaves, sliced tomatoes, and a drizzle of olive oil*
- **Pepperoni Delight:** *Sliced pepperoni, black olives, and a sprinkle of oregano*
- **Veggie Supreme:** *Mushrooms, bell peppers, red onion, spinach, and olives*
- **Barbecue Chicken:** *Shredded cooked chicken, barbecue sauce, red onions, and cilantro*
- **Hawaiian Twist:** *Pineapple, ham, and a handful of arugula for a peppery bite*
- **Breakfast Pizza:** *Scrambled eggs, crumbled bacon, and a drizzle of hot sauce*

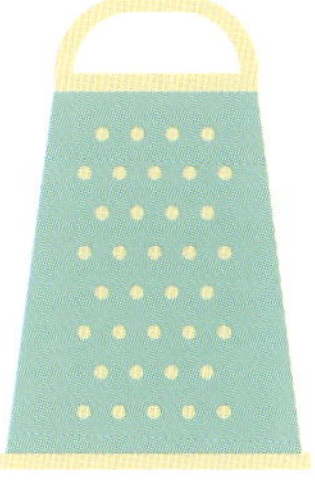

SPUDTACULAR BAKED POTATOES

Baked potatoes cooked over a campfire are a simple, hearty, and endlessly customizable meal. They can be a blank canvas for a variety of toppings, making them perfect for using leftovers or creating fun flavor combinations.

Large russet potatoes (1 per person)
Olive oil or butter
Salt and pepper
Cheddar cheese, shredded
Hot chili (homemade or canned)
Bacon crumbles
Sour cream
Green onions, chopped

1. Scrub the potatoes clean and pat dry.

2. Pierce each potato a few times with a fork to release steam.

3. Rub the potatoes with olive oil, then sprinkle generously with salt and pepper.

4. Wrap each potato tightly in a double layer of aluminum foil to protect them from burning.

5. Place the wrapped potatoes directly on hot coals or set them on a grate above the flames.

6. Turn them occasionally to ensure even cooking.

7. Cook for 40 to 60 minutes, depending on the size of the potato. You'll know they're done when a fork easily pierces through the center.

8. Serve with cheese, chili, bacon, sour cream, and green onions.

TOPPINGS

- **Pizza Potato:** *marinara or pizza sauce, shredded mozzarella cheese, pepperoni or sausage crumbles, black olives, diced peppers, mushrooms*
- **Barbecue Pulled Pork Potato:** *warm pulled pork, barbecue sauce, pickled onions or jalapeños*
- **Steakhouse Potato:** *sliced or chopped leftover steak, sautéed mushrooms and onions, blue cheese crumbles or shredded cheese, sour cream*
- **Tex-Mex Potato:** *seasoned ground beef or shredded chicken, black beans or refried beans, salsa or pico de gallo, sour cream, chopped cilantro*

PRO TIPS FOR CAMPFIRE COOKING

- **Precook:** *Parboil potatoes at home, then finish on the campfire to reduce cooking time.*
- **Make a toppings bar:** *Set up a DIY station so everyone can customize their potato.*
- **Keep hot:** *Wrap cooked potatoes in foil and a towel to stay warm while everyone tops their own.*

THE ULTIMATE CAMPFIRE BURGER

Grilled over an open fire, this burger captures smoky, charred flavors that can't be replicated on a stovetop. Combined with unique toppings and a touch of campfire magic, this burger is as unforgettable as the stories told around the flames.

FOR THE BURGER

1 1/2 pounds 80/20 ground beef (or freshly ground brisket/chuck mix for extra flavor)
1 teaspoon kosher salt
1/2 teaspoon freshly ground black pepper
1 teaspoon Worcestershire sauce
1/2 teaspoon smoked paprika
1/2 teaspoon garlic powder
1/4 teaspoon chili powder
1 tablespoon avocado oil or canola oil
4 slices smoked Gouda or sharp cheddar cheese

FOR THE BURGER BUILD

Butter
4 brioche or pretzel buns (buttered and fire-toasted)
4 tablespoons Garlic Aioli (page 142)
Fresh arugula or butter lettuce
Smoky Onion Jam (page 146)
8 slices thick-cut bacon, cooked over the fire until crispy
4 slices heirloom tomato
Pickled jalapeños (optional for a spicy kick)

1. Mix the ground beef with salt, pepper, Worcestershire sauce, smoked paprika, garlic powder, and chili powder. Divide into 4 portions and shape into patties, creating a small dimple in the center to prevent puffing.

2. Brush the grill grate with oil to prevent sticking.

3. Place the patties directly over the open flames or hot coals. Grill for 3 to 4 minutes per side for a medium doneness, flipping once.

4. During the last minute of cooking, top each patty with a slice of smoked Gouda or cheddar and let it melt.

5. Butter the brioche buns and toast them cut-side-down directly on the grill grate until golden and slightly charred. Set aside.

6. Spread garlic aioli on the bottom toasted bun.

7. Add a layer of arugula, followed by the cheesy burger patty.

8. Spoon a generous portion of the Smoky Onion Jam on top of the burger.

9. Top with crispy bacon slices, a thick slice of heirloom tomato, and a few pickled jalapeños if using.

10. Finish with the toasted top bun and press gently to hold it all together.

11. Serve the burgers immediately, wrapped in parchment or butcher paper for a rustic touch. Pair with fire-roasted potatoes or grilled corn for the ultimate campfire feast.

ON THE SIDE

STEAKHOUSE ROASTED VEGETABLES

Packed with flavor and perfectly caramelized, these steakhouse-style roasted vegetables are an ideal side dish or even a hearty main course for camping. The mix of smoky seasonings and herbs makes them stand out, and the method ensures they're easy to prepare outdoors.

2 large carrots, peeled and sliced into thick sticks
2 medium zucchini, sliced into thick rounds
1 large red bell pepper, cut into large chunks
1 large yellow onion, cut into wedges
1 (8-ounce) package baby bella mushrooms, halved
1 cup cherry tomatoes (optional, for a burst of sweetness)
2 tablespoons olive oil
1 teaspoon smoked paprika
1 teaspoon garlic powder
1 teaspoon dried thyme or rosemary
Salt and pepper to taste
1 tablespoon balsamic vinegar (optional, for added depth)
Chopped fresh parsley, for garnish

CAMPFIRE PREPARATION

1. Build a medium-hot campfire with a grate for grilling or use hot coals for even cooking. Or preheat a covered grill.

FOR THE VEGETABLES

1. In a large bowl or resealable bag, combine the carrots, zucchini, bell pepper, onion, mushrooms, and cherry tomatoes if using.

2. Drizzle with olive oil and toss or shake to coat.

3. Sprinkle with smoked paprika, garlic powder, thyme, and salt and pepper. Add balsamic vinegar, if using, and toss again.

4. Divide the seasoned vegetables evenly onto large sheets of heavy-duty aluminum foil. Fold the foil over and seal tightly to create packets. Double wrap with a second sheet of foil.

5. Place the foil packets directly on the hot grill grate or over medium-hot coals. Cook for 20 to 25 minutes, flipping the packets halfway through, until the vegetables are tender and slightly caramelized.

6. Open the packets carefully to avoid steam. Transfer the vegetables to a serving platter or enjoy straight from the foil. Sprinkle with fresh parsley for a bright finish.

TIPS

- *Serve alongside grilled steak, chicken, or fish, or enjoy as a main dish with crusty bread or quinoa for a complete meal.*
- *Sprinkle shredded Parmesan or crumbled feta over the veggies after cooking for extra richness.*
- *Add a handful of chopped nuts like walnuts or pecans for a nutty contrast.*
- *Use other favorite vegetables—broccoli, Brussels sprouts, or asparagus all work beautifully.*

LOADED POTATO SALAD

Packed with classic loaded baked potato flavors, this creamy potato salad is always a hit at potlucks. It's easy to prepare ahead of time. This recipe can be made ahead and travels well.

- 3 pounds red or Yukon Gold potatoes, washed and cut into bite-size pieces
- 1 cup sour cream
- 1/2 cup mayonnaise
- 1 tablespoon Dijon mustard
- 1 teaspoon garlic powder
- 1 teaspoon onion powder
- 1/2 teaspoon smoked paprika
- 1/2 teaspoon salt
- 1/4 teaspoon pepper
- 6 slices cooked bacon, crumbled
- 1 cup shredded sharp cheddar cheese
- 3 green onions, thinly sliced

1. Bring a large pot of salted water to a boil, and boil potatoes until fork-tender, about 10 to 15 minutes. Drain and let cool slightly.

2. In a large bowl, mix sour cream, mayonnaise, Dijon mustard, garlic powder, onion powder, smoked paprika, and salt and pepper until smooth.

3. Add the cooked potatoes, bacon, cheese, and green onions to the dressing. Gently toss to coat evenly.

4. Chill in the refrigerator for at least 1 hour before serving to allow the flavors to meld.

OPTIONAL ADD-INS

- *Chopped dill pickles or relish for a tangy twist.*
- *A handful of diced jalapeños for spice.*
- *Purple onions for some zip.*
- *Fresh herbs like dill or parsley for added freshness.*

With everything at her fingertips, meal time is an easy-time for the trailer home-maker.

Kitchen and dinette scenes these, with modern, built-in table units for easy serving. Every trailer appears more modern and effective if simply designed dishes and ornaments are combined with linens in harmonizing colors.

HAWAIIAN MACARONI SALAD

This macaroni salad is simple and easy to assemble but full of flavor. Be sure to keep well refrigerated before serving as the recipe contains mayonnaise.

SALAD

1 pound elbow macaroni
2 tablespoons apple cider vinegar
2 to 3 carrots, shredded
1/4 cup shredded onion

DRESSING

2 1/2 cups mayonnaise
1/4 cup milk
2 teaspoons sugar
Salt and pepper to taste

FOR THE SALAD

1. Cook macaroni according to package directions. Do not overcook. Rinse under cold water until completely cool to stop the cooking. Drain well and place in a bowl large enough to incorporate all ingredients.

2. Distribute the vinegar over the macaroni and add the carrots and onion. Lightly toss and refrigerate while you make the dressing or until the macaroni is thoroughly cooled.

FOR THE DRESSING

1. In a medium bowl, whisk together the mayonnaise, milk, and sugar. Gently fold the dressing into the salad until the macaroni is evenly coated. Season with salt and pepper to taste.

2. Cover and refrigerate for at least 4 hours. Overnight is best. Before serving, stir and add a little milk if you need to loosen it up. It shouldn't need more than a tablespoon. Adjust the seasoning if needed but be careful not to oversalt. A little goes a long way.

3. Serve with an ice cream scoop for authenticity and portion control.

➣ **Variations:** *Add peas, bay shrimp, or crab.*

CONFETTI COLESLAW

This spin on coleslaw is a healthier alternative to a mayonnaise version. The carrots and purple cabbage make it pop with lots of color. Add the jalapeño if you want a little bit of spice.

SLAW

- 1/2 head purple cabbage, shredded (about 3 cups)
- 1/2 head green cabbage, shredded (about 3 cups)
- 2 heaping cups shredded carrots
- 1 cup finely chopped cilantro
- 1/2 cup sliced green onion
- 1 jalapeño, seeded and finely diced (optional)

DRESSING

- 3 tablespoons extra-virgin olive oil
- 2 tablespoons apple cider vinegar
- 2 teaspoons sugar
- 1 to 2 cloves garlic, pressed
- Salt and pepper to taste

1. Combine the purple cabbage, green cabbage, carrots, cilantro, green onion, and jalapeño (if using) in a large bowl.

2. In a small bowl, whisk together the olive oil, vinegar, sugar, and garlic for the dressing. Fold the dressing into the slaw and toss to combine. Add salt and pepper to taste. Cover and refrigerate for at least an hour before serving.

COWBOY COLESLAW

It doesn't get much quicker or easier than this one. If you forgot to bring a potluck dish or need a quick side for your barbecue, this recipe is good in a pinch. The apples and cranberries give it some tartness, and candied walnuts or pecans give it a nutty crunch.

1 bag shredded cabbage
1 apple, chopped
1 (3.5-ounce) bag dried cranberries with glazed walnuts
½ (12-ounce) jar Marie's Coleslaw Dressing

In a large bowl, toss together cabbage, apple, cranberries and walnuts, and dressing. Serve immediately.

Contributed by Sheryl Hagen

SOUTHERN SLAW

Fresh, tangy, and sweet, this slaw is easy to make and pairs well with so many main dishes.

1 1/2 heads cabbage, shredded
1/2 cup vegetable oil
3 tablespoons sugar
3 tablespoons apple cider vinegar
2 tablespoons ketchup
1 tablespoon lemon juice
1/2 medium onion, peeled and cut into chucks
1/2 teaspoon salt
1 teaspoon paprika

1. Place shredded cabbage in a large mixing bowl and set aside.

2. Add oil, sugar, vinegar, ketchup, lemon juice, onion, salt, and paprika to a blender. Blend until smooth and pour over cabbage. Mix to coat.

3. Chill in the fridge for 30 minutes before serving.

Contributed by Wendy Cook

IT'S CURTAIN TIME FOR
UNIVERSAL TRAILERS
LOS ANGELES
The Big Scoop of '49
PRODUCED BY
UNIVERSAL
STARRING—Not One—but THREE sensational new models
FEATURING—The fascinating VIEW-look
ACT 1—At your Local Dealer Display
ACT 2—The Beauty Spot in Any Trailer Park
FINALE—UNIVERSAL, the Home Beautiful
INTRODUCING
The UNIVERSAL DeLuxe Model 31, peer of luxurious trailerhomes.
For years UNIVERSAL has set the pace in modern design, home appeal, and roamability. In maintaining this valued reputation, the new UNIVERSAL models go far beyond mere improvement. They are the "something really different" you have been waiting for.
TCMA
Member TCA
UNIVERSAL TRAILER CORP.
15220 S. Lakewood Blvd., Paramount, Calif., TOrrey 7-4606—7-3820
CHICAGO PLANT: 4884 N. Clark St., Chicago, Illinois

MARTI'S BLT MACARONI SALAD

The fresh parsley in this salad brings brightness to the dish—adding a light, refreshing touch similar to lemon juice, lemon zest, or vinegar.

- 1/2 cup mayonnaise
- 1/4 cup sour cream
- 2 tablespoons Dijon mustard
- 1 tablespoon apple cider vinegar
- 1 teaspoon honey
- Salt and pepper to taste
- 8 ounces elbow macaroni (cooked al dente, drained, and cooled)
- 6 slices bacon, cooked crisp and crumbled
- 1 cup cherry tomatoes (or chopped ripe tomatoes)
- 2 cups chopped lettuce (iceberg, romaine, or a mix of both)
- 2 green onions, thinly sliced
- 1/4 cup fresh chopped parsley
- 1 ripe but firm avocado, diced (optional)

1. Combine the mayonnaise, sour cream, Dijon mustard, apple cider vinegar, and honey in a large bowl. Whisk well and add salt and pepper to taste.

2. Add the macaroni, bacon, tomatoes, lettuce, onion, parsley, and avocado if using. Mix to coat with the dressing.

3. Adjust seasoning as needed before serving.

Contributed by Marti Domyancic

TIP

Flat-leaf and curly parsley can be eaten raw in salads. Flat-leaf parsley, also called Italian parsley, has a stronger flavor and smoother texture than curly parsley and is easier to clean. You can add it to salads chopped or thinly sliced (chiffonade).

HAPPY CAMPER CAESAR SALAD

Here's a classic Caesar salad recipe that balances tangy, creamy, and savory flavors with a satisfying crunch. The homemade croutons elevate the salad—if possible, don't skip this step!

FOR THE DRESSING

1 egg yolk*
1 teaspoon Dijon mustard
2 to 3 anchovy fillets** or 1 teaspoon anchovy paste
1 garlic clove, minced
2 tablespoons fresh lemon juice
1 teaspoon Worcestershire sauce
1/3 cup extra-virgin olive oil
2 tablespoons grated Parmesan cheese
Salt and freshly ground black pepper to taste

FOR THE CROUTONS

2 to 3 slices bread, preferably day-old
Splash olive oil
Pinch garlic powder
Pinch salt

FOR THE SALAD

1 large head romaine lettuce, washed, dried, and torn into bite-sized pieces
1/2 cup freshly grated Parmesan cheese
1 cup croutons***

MAKE THE DRESSING

1. In a medium bowl, whisk together the egg yolk, Dijon mustard, anchovies, garlic, lemon juice, and Worcestershire sauce until smooth.

2. Gradually whisk in the olive oil in a steady stream until the dressing is thick and emulsified.

3. Stir in the grated Parmesan and season with salt and pepper to taste.

MAKE THE CROUTONS

1. Preheat oven to 375 degrees F.

2. Cut the bread into cubes.

3. Toss with olive oil, garlic powder, and salt.

4. Spread on a baking sheet and bake for 10 to 12 minutes or until golden and crisp.

ASSEMBLE THE SALAD

1. Place the romaine lettuce in a large serving bowl.

2. Toss with the dressing until evenly coated.

3. Sprinkle with grated Parmesan and croutons.

4. Serve immediately.

**2 tablespoons mayonnaise may be substituted as a safer option*

***Optional, but traditional*

****Packaged croutons may be substituted but homemade are preferred for extra flavor*

VARIATIONS

- *For added protein, top with grilled chicken, shrimp, or hard-boiled eggs.*
- *For a twist, add bacon crumbles or avocado slices.*

THREE-BEAN SALAD

This colorful salad makes a filling side dish for burgers, hot dogs, grilled chicken, barbecue, Sloppy Joes, and more. It's great to make ahead as it travels well.

1 (16-ounce) can green beans, drained
1 (16-ounce) can kidney beans, drained
1 (16-ounce) can garbanzo beans, drained
1/4 cup extra-virgin olive oil
1/4 cup apple cider vinegar
2 garlic cloves, minced or grated
1 teaspoon Dijon mustard
1/2 teaspoon honey
1 teaspoon salt
1/2 teaspoon pepper
1/4 cup chopped parsley for garnish (optional)

1. Combine the green beans, kidney beans, and garbanzo beans in a large bowl and toss gently to combine.

2. In a small bowl, whisk together olive oil, apple cider vinegar, garlic, Dijon mustard, honey, salt, and pepper. Pour over bean salad and toss to coat. Sprinkle with parsley if using. Chill for 1 hour or overnight.

MID-CENTURY LIME GELATIN MOLD

This classic Jell-O mold recipe was a staple at mid-century dinner parties and potlucks, beloved for its bright color, refreshing taste, and whimsical presentation. It's a true retro treat that's as fun to make as it is to eat.

- 1 (3-ounce) package lime-flavored gelatin
- 1 cup boiling water
- 1 cup cold water
- 1 (8-ounce) can crushed pineapple, undrained
- 1/2 cup small-curd cottage cheese
- 1/2 cup mayonnaise
- 1/4 teaspoon salt
- 1 cup whipped topping or heavy cream, whipped
- 1/2 cup chopped walnuts or pecans (optional)
- Extra whipped topping or whipped cream, chopped nuts, and pineapple ring for serving (optional)

1. In a medium mixing bowl, dissolve the lime gelatin in 1 cup of boiling water, stirring until completely dissolved. Add the cold water and stir well.

2. Stir in the crushed pineapple, including the juice. Chill the mixture in the refrigerator for 30 to 45 minutes or until it reaches the consistency of unbeaten egg whites.

3. In a separate bowl, combine the cottage cheese, mayonnaise, and salt. Gently fold in the whipped topping until smooth.

4. Fold the cottage cheese mixture into the slightly thickened gelatin. Stir in the chopped nuts, if desired.

5. Pour the mixture into a lightly greased or sprayed mold. Cover and refrigerate for at least 4 hours or until fully set.

6. To unmold, dip the mold briefly in warm water (about 10 seconds) and invert it onto a serving plate.

7. Garnish with a dollop of whipped topping and a sprinkle of chopped nuts or a pineapple ring for a truly nostalgic presentation.

THE DELUXE "APARTMENT" ON WHEELS

KOZY Coach

TRADE NAME REG. U.S. PAT. OFF.

Travel - wise tourists will tell you to look at the five Kozy Coach models before you buy.

Genuine coach value is determined by three factors: livability, roadability, and engineered construction for safety and long life. It will be a revelation to you to see how thoroughly these three factors have been considered in the Kozy Coach models shown in our new brochure. Send ten cents for a copy.

KOZY KOACH CO.

515 E. Michigan Ave.
Kalamazoo, Michigan

CAMP-STYLE GRILLED WINGS

These wings are perfect for camping, easy to prepare, and packed with flavor. Using a grill basket makes them a breeze to cook over a campfire or on a portable grill. If you're in an RV with electricity, an air fryer is a great alternative. You can season the wings and refrigerate them in a sealed container for up to 24 hours before cooking. This allows the flavors to marinate, making them even tastier!

- 3 pounds chicken wings, split into flats and drumettes
- 2 tablespoons olive oil
- 1 teaspoon garlic powder
- 1 teaspoon smoked paprika
- 1 teaspoon salt
- 1/2 teaspoon pepper
- 1/4 teaspoon cayenne pepper (optional for heat)
- Classic Buffalo Sauce (page 148)

TO PREPARE THE WINGS

1. Rinse the chicken wings and pat them dry with paper towels.

2. In a large bowl, whisk together olive oil, garlic powder, smoked paprika, salt, pepper, and cayenne pepper if using. Toss wings in the oil and spices to coat.

GRILL BASKET METHOD

1. Preheat your grill to medium-high heat (about 400 degrees F).

2. Place the seasoned wings in a grill basket in a single layer.

Continued →

3. Grill for 20 to 25 minutes, turning the basket every 5 to 7 minutes to ensure even cooking. Wings are done when they are golden and crispy, with an internal temperature of 165 degrees F.

AIR FRYER METHOD

1. Preheat the air fryer to 400 degrees F.

2. Arrange the wings in the air fryer basket in a single layer (cook in batches if needed).

3. Air fry for 18 to 20 minutes, shaking the basket halfway through, until the wings are crispy and fully cooked.

SERVING SUGGESTIONS

- *Serve with your favorite wing sauces like buffalo, barbecue, or honey mustard. Or try honey sriracha or garlic Parmesan for different, flavorful twists.*

- *Celery and carrot sticks with a side of ranch or blue cheese dressing for dipping make a great accompaniment.*

GLOBAL FLAVORS

Hot wings are definitely a timeless favorite, and recent food trends have put a creative twist on classic wings. Here are a few popular variations:

- **Korean Barbecue Wings:** *Coated in a sweet and savory gochujang glaze.*
- **Thai Peanut Wings:** *Tossed in a creamy peanut sauce with a hint of spice.*
- **Jerk Chicken Wings:** *Rubbed with Caribbean spices and grilled for a smoky flavor.*

GRILLED ELOTES-STYLE CORN

Elotes, or Mexican street corn, is a smoky, tangy, and slightly spicy treat that's perfect for cooking over a campfire. They are great as a side dish to grilled meat and tacos or as a stand-alone snack. This recipe transforms simple grilled corn into a flavorful side dish that everyone will rave about.

4 ears fresh corn, husked
2 tablespoons olive oil or melted butter
Salt to taste
1/2 cup mayonnaise
1/2 cup sour cream
1 tablespoon fresh-squeezed lime juice
1 cup crumbled cotija cheese, divided*
1 teaspoon chili powder
1/4 teaspoon smoked paprika (optional)
2 tablespoons chopped fresh cilantro
1 lime, cut into wedges

PREPARE THE CAMPFIRE

1. Set up a campfire with medium-hot coals or use a grill grate over the fire.

2. Lightly coat each ear of corn with olive oil and season with a pinch of salt.

3. Place the corn directly on the grill grate or campfire grill over medium heat.

4. Turn the corn every 2 to 3 minutes until it's charred and tender, about 10 to 12 minutes.

PREPARE THE TOPPINGS

1. In a small bowl, mix the mayonnaise, sour cream, lime juice, and half of the crumbled cotija cheese until smooth.

2. In another small bowl, combine the chili powder and smoked paprika if using.

ASSEMBLE THE ELOTES

1. Remove the grilled corn from the heat and brush or slather each ear generously with the mayo-and-sour-cream mixture.

2. Sprinkle evenly with the chili powder mixture.

3. Roll the corn in the remaining cotija cheese to coat it.

4. Garnish with chopped cilantro and serve with lime wedges on the side for squeezing over the top.

**Feta may be substituted.*

TIPS FOR SUCCESS

- **Allow it to char:** *Don't shy away from letting the corn get a little blackened—it adds to the smoky flavor.*
- **Spice it up:** *Add a pinch of cayenne pepper for extra heat or drizzle with hot sauce for a fiery kick.*
- **Make a handle:** *Stick a wooden skewer or a sturdy stick into the base of each cob for a convenient handle.*

THE BEST-EVER JALAPEÑO POPPERS

Fancy up your steak or burger meal with these jalapeño poppers as a campfire appetizer.

12 large fresh jalapeños
1 (8-ounce) package cream cheese, softened
1 cup shredded sharp cheddar cheese
½ cup cooked and crumbled bacon (about 5 to 6 slices)
2 garlic cloves, minced
¼ teaspoon smoked paprika
¼ teaspoon pepper
½ teaspoon onion powder
½ cup panko breadcrumbs
2 tablespoons butter, melted
¼ cup grated Parmesan cheese
Chopped chives or parsley for garnish (optional)

1. Preheat your oven to 400 degrees F and line a baking sheet with parchment paper or aluminum foil for easy cleanup.

2. Cut the jalapeños in half lengthwise and scoop out the seeds and membranes with a spoon.

3. Combine the softened cream cheese, shredded cheddar, crumbled bacon, minced garlic, smoked paprika, pepper, and onion powder in a mixing bowl. Mix until well blended.

4. Stuff the jalapeños with the cream cheese mixture into each jalapeño half, pressing gently to fill completely. Place the stuffed jalapeños on the prepared baking sheet, cut-side up.

5. Mix the panko breadcrumbs, melted butter, and grated Parmesan cheese in a small bowl. Sprinkle a generous amount over each stuffed jalapeño for a golden, crispy topping.

6. Bake the jalapeños in the preheated oven for 18 to 20 minutes, or until the tops are golden and the cheese is bubbling.

7. Remove from the oven and let them cool for 5 minutes. Sprinkle with chopped chives for a fresh finishing touch if desired.

OPTIONAL ADD-ONS

- *For extra indulgence, wrap each stuffed jalapeño in a slice of thin bacon before baking. Use a toothpick to hold it in place and increase baking time by 5 to 7 minutes.*
- *Serve with a side of sriracha mayo or a drizzle of hot honey for a unique, sweet-spicy twist.*

DIPS AND SAUCES

7-LAYER BEAN DIP

A camping favorite, this classic bean dip can be made ahead and kept cold until serving.

- 2 (15-ounce) cans refried beans
- 1 (16-ounce) container sour cream
- 1 package taco seasoning mix
- 1½ cups shredded Mexican blend cheese
- 2 Roma tomatoes, diced
- 4 green onions, sliced
- 1 small can sliced olives, drained
- 2 avocados, peeled, pitted, and cubed

1. Spread the refried beans in the bottom of a 9 x 13-inch dish.

2. In a small bowl, mix together sour cream and taco seasoning mix. Using a spatula, spread the sour cream mixture over the refried beans.

3. Sprinkle with shredded cheese and top with tomatoes, onions, olives, and avocado.

"Trailer Camp Friendships," by Douglass Crockwell. Number 79 in the series "Home Life in America"

In this friendly, freedom-loving land of ours—Beer belongs . . . enjoy it!

BEER AND ALE—AMERICA'S BEVERAGES OF MODERATION
Sponsored by the United States Brewers Foundation . . . Chartered 1862

CAMPFIRE CHILI CHEESE DIP

This two-ingredient dip couldn't be simpler or more delicious. Make it ahead or simply pack the ingredients to whip up a quick and easy dip on the road that will fill you up. This dip can be served warm or cold.

1 (8-ounce) package cream cheese
1 (15-ounce) can chili (vegetarian or meat)
Tortilla chips for serving
Taco sauce for serving (optional)

1. Cut the cream cheese into about eight chunks and place in a medium saucepan over medium heat.

2. Add the can of chili to the saucepan and mix.

3. Heat until the cheese is melted and everything is warmed through.

4. Serve with tortilla chips and taco sauce, if desired.

Contributed by Toni Miltenberger

CREAMY SPINACH DIP

This classic spinach dip is great with crackers, bread, or fresh veggies.

1 cup sour cream
1 cup mayonnaise
1 (1.4-ounce) package vegetable soup mix
1 (10-ounce) package frozen chopped spinach, thawed and drained
2 green onions, thinly sliced
1 (8-ounce) can water chestnuts, drained and finely chopped (optional)

1. In a medium bowl, mix sour cream, mayonnaise, and soup mix until well combined.

2. Add spinach, green onions, and water chestnuts (if using). Stir gently until evenly mixed.

3. Cover and refrigerate for at least 2 hours or overnight to let the flavors meld.

Travelite
"HOMETTE"
First with Aluminum
NEW MODEL
"SIX-27"
Ample accommodations for a solo bachelor or a family of six...
● Completely re-designed inside and out, features of the new "627" include a new type of dormer construction which gives full head room for the entire length of the trailer, approximately 200 cubic feet of storage space, an upholstered pullman type lounge which converts into a double bed, and all modern furnishings. Floor length is 24 feet. Overall length approximately 27 feet.
Both the model 627 and the model 427 shown at the right are now equipped with an all-aluminum roof; exteriors on both are of aircraft aluminum.
"HOMETTE"
MODEL 427
Accommodates 4 persons in 3 luxurious rooms. Standard, De Luxe and Custom styles. Floor length 24 feet.
ON DISPLAY AT YOUR TRAVELITE DEALER or write for circular
Travelite Trailer Co.
4013-41 WENTWORTH AVE., CHICAGO 9, ILL. TELEPHONE DREXEL 1200
2730 BRYAN AVE., FORT WORTH 3, TEXAS TELEPHONE 4-3282

JALAPEÑO CHEDDAR DIP

Perfect as a dip for tortilla chips, crackers, or pretzels. It even works well as a burger topping.

1 cup mayonnaise
½ cup sour cream
¼ teaspoon garlic powder
¼ teaspoon onion powder
Pinch of cayenne pepper (optional)
2 cups shredded sharp cheddar cheese
2 to 3 fresh jalapeños, finely chopped (remove seeds for less heat)

1. In a medium bowl, mix mayonnaise, sour cream, garlic powder, onion powder, and cayenne pepper (if using).

2. Fold in cheddar cheese and jalapeños. Mix until well combined.

3. Transfer to an airtight container and chill for at least 2 hours or overnight.

FRENCH ONION DIP

A savory favorite that's easy to make and pairs well with potato chips, pita chips, or fresh veggies.

2 cups sour cream
1 (1-ounce) package French onion soup mix
1/2 teaspoon Worcestershire sauce
Pinch of black pepper
1 tablespoon finely chopped fresh parsley for garnish (optional)

1. In a medium bowl, mix sour cream, soup mix, Worcestershire sauce, and pepper until smooth.

2. Cover and refrigerate for at least 1 hour or overnight to let the flavors develop.

3. Before serving, stir well and garnish with parsley if desired.

GARLIC AIOLI

Garlic aioli is a deliciously creamy condiment that adds a burst of flavor to dishes. It's perfect as a dip for fries, a spread for sandwiches, or a topping for grilled meats and vegetables.

½ cup mayonnaise
2 to 3 cloves garlic, pressed
1 tablespoon lemon juice
½ teaspoon Dijon mustard
Salt and pepper to taste

1. *In a small bowl, combine the mayonnaise, garlic, lemon juice, and Dijon mustard. Feel free to add more garlic, if desired.*

2. *Mix well until all ingredients are thoroughly combined.*

3. *Season with salt and pepper to taste.*

4. *Cover the bowl and refrigerate for at least 30 minutes to allow the flavors to marry.*

VARIATIONS

- **Herb Aioli:** Add chopped fresh herbs like parsley, basil, or chives for a herb-infused flavor.
- **Spicy Aioli:** Mix in a pinch of cayenne pepper or a few dashes of hot sauce for a spicy kick.
- **Roasted Garlic Aioli:** Use roasted garlic instead of raw garlic for a milder, slightly sweet flavor.
- **Sun-Dried Tomato Aioli:** Blend in finely chopped sun-dried tomatoes for a tangy twist.

SERVING SUGGESTIONS

- *Serve with fries, sweet potato fries, or onion rings for a gourmet dipping experience.*
- *Spread on sandwiches or burgers instead of regular mayonnaise for added flavor.*
- *Use as a topping for grilled chicken, fish, or vegetables to enhance their taste.*

BACON JAM

Bacon jam is a savory-sweet spread that combines crispy bacon with caramelized onions, brown sugar, and a little vinegar for a rich, delicious topping.

1 pound thick-cut bacon, chopped
1 large yellow onion, finely chopped
2 cloves garlic, minced
½ teaspoon freshly ground black pepper
¼ teaspoon red pepper flakes (optional)
½ cup strong coffee or water (to deglaze)
¼ cup packed brown sugar
¼ cup maple syrup
¼ cup apple cider vinegar
1 tablespoon balsamic vinegar

1. In a large skillet, cook the chopped bacon over medium heat until it becomes crispy and golden, about 8 to 10 minutes. Stir occasionally to ensure even cooking. Remove bacon with a slotted spoon and set it aside. Remove excess bacon fat from the pan.

2. Add the onions to the same skillet and cook over medium-low heat for about 15 to 20 minutes, stirring frequently. The onions should become soft and caramelized, turning a deep golden brown.

3. Add the garlic and cook for 1 to 2 minutes more until fragrant. Stir in the pepper and red pepper flakes, if using.

4. Pour in the coffee to deglaze the pan, scraping up any browned bits stuck to the bottom. Add the brown sugar, maple syrup, apple cider vinegar, and balsamic vinegar. Stir well to combine.

5. Bring the mixture to a gentle simmer and cook for about 15 to 20 minutes, stirring occasionally. The sauce should thicken and become syrupy.

6. Once the mixture is thickened and reduced, add the cooked bacon back into the skillet. Stir to combine and cook for another 5 minutes to let the flavors meld together. If the jam gets too thick, add a little more coffee or water to reach your desired consistency.

7. Remove from heat and let the bacon jam cool. It will thicken further as it cools. Store in an airtight container in the fridge for up to 2 weeks.

Fig. 2. Pleasant Living.

SMOKY ONION JAM

An excellent topping for burgers, onion jam is also great in a grilled cheese sandwich, as a sauce for pork, or to spread on crostini or crackers.

2 tablespoons butter
2 large, sweet onions, thinly sliced
¼ teaspoon salt
1 tablespoon brown sugar
¼ teaspoon smoked paprika
2 tablespoons bourbon or water
1 teaspoon balsamic vinegar

1. In a cast-iron skillet over medium heat on an open fire, melt the butter. Add the sliced onions and salt, stirring occasionally, until onions are soft and caramelized (about 10 to 15 minutes).

2. Stir in the brown sugar, smoked paprika, and bourbon. Allow it to bubble for 2 minutes to cook off the alcohol if using bourbon.

3. Finish with a splash of balsamic vinegar, stirring the sauce until it is thick and jammy.

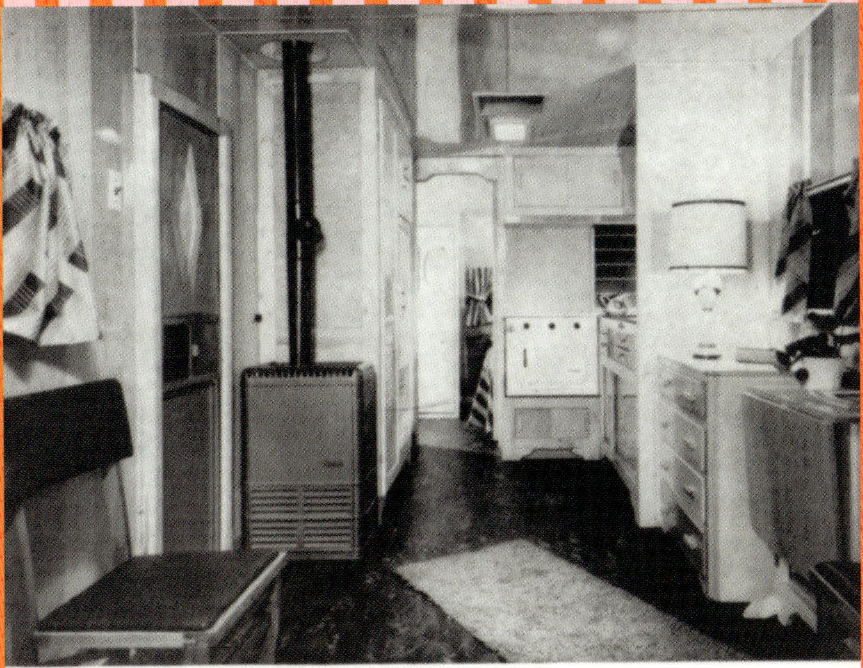

↑ LOOKING THROUGH LIVING ROOM, KITCHEN AND BEDROOM ↓WELL APPOINTED KITCHEN

CLASSIC BUFFALO SAUCE

This zesty sauce is the ultimate companion for wings. It's quick and easy to make, with just a handful of ingredients.

1/4 cup unsalted butter
1/2 cup hot sauce (such as Frank's RedHot)
1 tablespoon white vinegar
1/2 teaspoon garlic powder
1/4 teaspoon Worcestershire sauce
1/4 teaspoon cayenne pepper (optional)

1. In a small saucepan over low heat, melt the butter, stirring gently to avoid browning.

2. Stir in the hot sauce, vinegar, garlic powder, and Worcestershire sauce. If you like extra heat, add the cayenne pepper.

3. Simmer the sauce for 2 to 3 minutes, stirring occasionally, until it's smooth and slightly thickened.

4. Toss cooked wings in the warm sauce until evenly coated or serve it as a dipping sauce.

BRAZILIAN-INSPIRED CHIMICHURRI

A Brazilian-inspired twist on chimichurri incorporates tropical and smoky flavors, creating a bold companion for various cuts of meat. It's the perfect addition to your next cookout and will impress your guests with its vibrant taste and aromatic punch.

1 cup finely chopped fresh parsley
½ cup finely chopped fresh cilantro
2 garlic cloves, minced
1 small red chili, seeded and finely chopped*
1 teaspoon smoked paprika
½ teaspoon ground cumin
½ teaspoon salt
¼ teaspoon black pepper
¼ cup olive oil
3 tablespoons red wine vinegar
Juice of 1 lime

1. Combine the parsley, cilantro, garlic, and chili in a medium bowl.

2. Add smoked paprika, cumin, salt, and black pepper. Mix well.

3. Whisk in olive oil, red wine vinegar, and lime juice until combined. Adjust seasoning to taste.

4. Cover and let the flavors meld for at least 30 minutes. The sauce can be made up to a day ahead and refrigerated.

**½ teaspoon red pepper flakes may be substituted for less heat.*

THIS CHIMICHURRI IS VERSATILE AND COMPLEMENTS VARIOUS MEATS, INCLUDING

- **Beef:** *picanha, skirt steak, flank steak, rib eye*
- **Chicken:** *boneless thighs and drumsticks*
- **Pork:** *tenderloin, ribs, pork chops*
- **Lamb:** *loin chops, leg steaks*

WHAT'S FOR DESSERT?

CAFÉ PAULO CARROT CAKE

Before my vintage trailer days, I owned a coffee shop in Chico, California, where our carrot cake was a crowd favorite. We baked it in large sheet trays and froze it, pulling out serving-sized pieces as needed. You can do the same: make this treat ahead, freeze it, and set it out the night before for a perfect pairing with a cup of coffee. And because I'm not a fan of walnuts, we left them out of our recipe at the café!

CAKE

1 1/2 cups sugar
1/2 cup vegetable oil
1/2 cup applesauce
3 eggs
2 cups all-purpose flour
2 teaspoons cinnamon
1 teaspoon baking soda
1 teaspoon vanilla
1/2 teaspoon salt
3 cups shredded carrots (about 5 medium)
3/4 cup raisins
1/2 cup shredded coconut
3/4 cup chopped walnuts (optional)

CREAM CHEESE FROSTING

1 (8-ounce) package cream cheese, softened
1/4 cup butter, softened
2 to 3 teaspoons milk
1 teaspoon vanilla
4 cups powdered sugar

FOR THE CAKE

1. Preheat the oven to 350 degrees F. Grease the bottom and sides of a 9 x 13-inch pan with shortening, then lightly flour.

2. In a large bowl, use an electric mixer on low speed to blend the sugar, oil, applesauce, and eggs until combined, about 30 seconds.

3. Add the flour, cinnamon, baking soda, vanilla, and salt, and beat on low for another minute.

4. Fold in the carrots, raisins, coconut, and nuts if using, then pour the batter into the prepared pan.

5. Bake for 40 to 45 minutes or until a toothpick inserted in the center comes out clean.

6. Cool the cake in the pan on a cooling rack.

FOR THE FROSTING

1. In a medium bowl, combine cream cheese, butter, milk, and vanilla with an electric mixer on low speed until smooth. Gradually beat in powdered sugar, 1 cup at a time, on low speed until smooth and spreadable.

2. Frost the cooled cake and cut it into roughly 3-inch squares.

3. Wrap individual servings in plastic wrap.

4. Freeze or keep chilled for up to 5 days. Serve at room temperature.

BLISSFUL BREAD PUDDING

Bread pudding is one of those recipes that make the most of your leftovers while delivering cozy, campfire-ready flavors. Whether you're flipping French toast or slow-cooking pudding, your crew will be asking for more.

6 to 8 leftover hot dog or hamburger buns*
3 large eggs
2 cups milk**
1/2 cup sugar
1 teaspoon pure vanilla extract
1 teaspoon cinnamon
1/4 teaspoon nutmeg
2 tablespoons butter, melted
1/2 cup raisins (soaked in warm water or rum for extra flavor)
1/4 cup chopped nuts or chocolate chips (optional)

1. Cut the buns into 1-inch cubes.

2. In a large bowl, whisk together eggs, milk, sugar, vanilla, cinnamon, nutmeg, and melted butter. Add the bread cubes and toss until evenly coated. Let sit for 15 to 20 minutes for the bread to absorb the mixture.

3. Stir in the soaked raisins and nuts, if using.

4. Grease the inside of a Dutch oven. Pour in the bread mixture, spreading evenly.

5. Cover and place over hot coals, with additional coals on the lid. Cook for 30 to 40 minutes, checking occasionally to ensure it doesn't burn. The bread pudding is done when the center is set, and the top is golden.

6. To serve, drizzle with a powdered sugar, milk, and vanilla glaze or enjoy warm with whipped cream or ice cream.

* *Any leftover bread will work.*

** *Use half-and-half for a creamier pudding.*

BEST-EVER PINEAPPLE UPSIDE-DOWN CAKE

This recipe combines classic flavors with a perfectly moist, buttery cake. It's rich in brown sugar caramel topping and features the iconic pineapple rings and cherries that make this dessert a timeless favorite. Transport your taste buds back to classic comfort food bliss.

TOPPING

- 1/2 cup unsalted butter, melted
- 1 cup packed light brown sugar
- 1 (20-ounce) can pineapple rings in juice, drained (reserve 1/4 cup juice)
- 10 to 12 maraschino cherries

CAKE

- 1 3/4 cups all-purpose flour
- 1 1/2 teaspoons baking powder
- 1/2 teaspoon baking soda
- 1/2 teaspoon salt
- 1/2 cup unsalted butter, softened
- 3/4 cup granulated sugar
- 1/4 cup packed light brown sugar
- 2 large eggs
- 1 teaspoon pure vanilla extract
- 1/2 cup sour cream or plain Greek yogurt
- 1/4 cup reserved pineapple juice

FOR THE TOPPING

1. Preheat oven to 350 degrees F. Generously grease a 9-inch round cake pan and line the bottom with parchment paper for easier release.

2. Pour the melted butter evenly into the prepared pan. Sprinkle the brown sugar over the butter to form a thick, even layer. Arrange the pineapple rings over the sugar, fitting them snugly. Place a cherry in the center of each ring and in any gaps between rings.

Continued →

FOR THE CAKE

1. In a medium bowl, whisk together the flour, baking powder, baking soda, and salt. Set aside.

2. In a large mixing bowl, beat the softened butter, sugar, and brown sugar with an electric mixer until light and fluffy, about 2 to 3 minutes.

3. Beat in the eggs, one at a time, until fully incorporated. Mix in the vanilla and sour cream until smooth.

4. Gradually add the dry ingredients to the wet mixture in three additions, alternating with the reserved pineapple juice. Begin and end with the dry ingredients. Mix until just combined—do not overmix.

5. Carefully pour and spread the cake batter over the pineapple topping in the pan, smoothing it out evenly. Bake for 40 to 45 minutes, or until the top is golden and a toothpick inserted in the center comes out clean.

6. Allow the cake to cool in the pan for 10 to 15 minutes. Run a knife around the edges to loosen and then place a serving platter upside-down over the pan. Quickly and carefully invert the cake onto the platter. Lift the pan off gently.

7. Let the cake cool slightly before serving. Slice and enjoy while warm or at room temperature.

8. Store leftovers in an airtight container at room temperature for up to 2 days or refrigerate for up to 5 days.

- *For a deeper caramel flavor, use dark brown sugar for the topping.*
- *Use the reserved pineapple juice to boost the cake's flavor and moisture.*

CLASSIC VANILLA ICE CREAM

There's something magical about making your own ice cream, especially on a camping trip. The anticipation of waiting for it to churn, the fun of taking turns cranking the handle or watching an electric maker do the hard work, and the reward of that first creamy scoop.

Making ice cream is a nostalgic nod to simpler times, and it's a great way to bring family and friends together. This basic vanilla recipe is perfect on its own but can be transformed with easy add-ins to satisfy every sweet tooth.

4 cups heavy cream
4 cups whole milk
2 cups granulated sugar
2 tablespoons pure vanilla extract
$\frac{1}{4}$ teaspoon salt

1. In a large mixing bowl, whisk together the cream, milk, sugar, vanilla, and salt until the sugar is dissolved.

2. Pour the mixture into the canister of a 4-quart ice cream maker.

3. Follow the manufacturer's instructions for your machine. If using a hand-crank machine, let the kids help out! The churning takes about 30 to 40 minutes, depending on your maker.

4. Once churned, transfer the ice cream to a container and freeze for 2 to 4 hours to firm up, or enjoy immediately as soft serve.

FUN FLAVOR ADD-INS

Take your vanilla ice cream to the next level! There's no wrong way to enjoy this ice cream. Whether you keep it simple with vanilla or jazz it up with fun flavors, every scoop will be a delicious memory in the making.

Chocolate Dream

1. Whisk 1/2 cup cocoa powder into the milk and sugar mixture before churning.

2. For a richer flavor, add 1/2 cup melted and cooled dark chocolate.

Peanut Butter Bliss

1. Swirl in 1 cup of creamy peanut butter after churning.

2. Top with a drizzle of strawberry jelly or fresh strawberry slices for a PB&J twist.

Salted Caramel Swirl

1. Fold in 1/2 cup caramel sauce and a pinch of sea salt after churning.

2. Add toasted pecans or chocolate chips for extra texture.

Cookies Galore

1. Mix in 1 cup of crushed chocolate sandwich cookies, sugar cookies, or even chunks of cookie dough for a decadent treat.

WHADINGER DESSERT BISCUITS

Whadinger biscuits are fun to make. These delicious, hollowed-out bread shells can be filled with sweet or savory ingredients.

Whadinger Stick (page 27)
Butter or cooking spray for greasing
1 can of refrigerated biscuit dough (such as Pillsbury)
Optional fillings (see ideas below)

1. Lightly grease the foil-covered end of your Whadinger stick with butter.

2. Flatten a biscuit slightly with your hands and wrap it around the foil-covered end of the stick. Stretch and pinch the dough to seal the edges, creating a hollow, cuplike shape. Ensure the dough is evenly distributed to avoid burning.

3. Hold the stick over glowing embers (not direct flames) and rotate it slowly to cook the biscuit evenly. This will take 8 to 12 minutes. The biscuit is done when it's golden brown and easily slides off the stick.

4. Let the biscuit cool slightly before filling it with your favorite ingredients.

SWEET WHADINGER FILLINGS

- **Campfire S'mores:** *Fill with mini marshmallows, chocolate chips, and crushed graham crackers.*
- **Pie Pockets:** *Add canned apple, cherry, or blueberry pie filling and a dollop of whipped cream.*
- **Berry Cheesecake:** *Combine cream cheese, fresh berries, and a drizzle of honey.*
- **Peanut Butter and Banana:** *Spread peanut butter inside and top with banana slices and a drizzle of chocolate syrup.*

APPLE DUMP CAKE

There's nothing quite like the comfort of a warm dessert after a day of adventuring. This easy, no-fuss recipe is easy to whip up in your RV oven or over the coals in a Dutch oven. It combines the cozy flavors of spiced apples with a buttery, crumbly topping. Plus, the aroma of cinnamon and baked apples will make your RV or campsite feel like home.

2 (14-ounce) cans apple pie filling
1 box yellow cake mix
1/2 cup butter
Vanilla ice cream for serving (optional)

1. Spray a Dutch oven with cooking spray or line it with parchment paper to ease in cleanup.

2. Dump the pie filling into the bottom of a 12-inch Dutch oven.

3. Dump the cake mix over the filling and spread out evenly, but do not mix.

4. Cut the butter in slices and place over the top of the cake mix.

5. Cover and bake at 350 degrees F for about one hour. You will know it's ready when you can smell the aroma of the apple and cake. A toothpick inserted in the center should come out clean.

6. Serve warm, topped with vanilla ice cream if you like.

Variation: *Replace the apple pie filling for cherry and the yellow cake mix with chocolate.*

Contributed by Patti Holroyd

BAKING IN A DUTCH OVEN OVER COALS

To achieve a 350 degree F temperature in a Dutch oven using coals, place roughly twice the diameter of your Dutch oven in charcoal briquettes, with about two-thirds of them on the lid and one-third underneath. For a 12-inch Dutch oven, this would mean using 24 briquettes with 16 on top and 8 below.

The number of coals needed will directly correlate with the size of your Dutch oven. For most baking recipes, place more coals on the lid than underneath to ensure even heat distribution. Always monitor your cooking temperature and adjust the coal placement if necessary.

BROWN BUTTER SALTED CHOCOLATE CHIP COOKIES

These cookies have a cult following for a reason—they're a perfect balance of nutty brown butter, gooey chocolate, and a hint of sea salt. A frequent winner at cookie competitions, this recipe elevates the classic chocolate chip cookie into a showstopping treat.

1 cup unsalted butter
2 1/4 cups all-purpose flour
1 teaspoon baking soda
1/2 teaspoon salt
3/4 cup packed dark brown sugar
1/2 cup sugar
2 large eggs
2 teaspoons pure vanilla extract
1 1/2 to 2 cups semi-sweet or dark chocolate chunks (or a mix of both)
Flaky sea salt, for garnish

1. Brown the butter by melting it in a medium saucepan over medium heat, stirring constantly, until it turns golden and develops a nutty aroma, which takes about 4 to 5 minutes. Pour into a heatproof bowl and let it cool slightly.

2. In a medium bowl, whisk together the flour, baking soda, and salt, then set aside.

3. In a large mixing bowl, combine the browned butter, brown sugar, and sugar, beating until smooth and creamy. Add the eggs one at a time, mixing well after each addition. Stir in the vanilla. Gradually mix in the dry ingredients until just combined. Fold in the chocolate chunks.

4. Cover the dough and refrigerate it for at least 1 hour, or up to 24 hours.

5. Preheat the oven to 350 degrees F. Line baking sheets with parchment paper. Scoop balls of dough about 2 tablespoons each onto the baking sheets, sprinkle each with flaky sea salt, and bake

for 10 to 12 minutes until the edges are golden and the centers are just set. Allow cookies to cool for 5 minutes on the baking sheet before transferring to a wire rack.

- *Chilling the dough is key—it deepens the flavor and ensures a chewy texture with crisp edges.*
- *For extra decadence, press a few additional chocolate chunks into the top of each cookie as they come out of the oven.*

CAMPFIRE BANANA BOATS

A perfect dessert for cozy nights around the campfire, this nostalgic treat is simple, delicious, and customizable. Add a scoop of vanilla ice cream for a truly indulgent finish.

1 banana
1 to 2 tablespoons of butter or margarine
1 tablespoon light brown sugar
1/4 teaspoon cinnamon
Splash of dark rum or brandy (optional)

1. Slice the banana lengthwise, keeping the peel intact if desired, or remove it for a softer texture.

2. Place the banana on a large sheet of heavy-duty aluminum foil, enough to wrap it into a pocket.

3. Add the butter and sprinkle with brown sugar and cinnamon. Drizzle with rum if using.

4. Fold the foil into a secure pocket, with the seam on top and the ends tightly wrapped to prevent leaks.

5. Place the packet directly in your firepit or on a grate. Cook for 10 to 15 minutes, until the butter and sugar caramelize and the banana becomes soft but not mushy. Use tongs to lift and lightly shake the packet occasionally to prevent burning.

6. Carefully open the foil pocket (watch out for steam!) and enjoy the banana straight from the foil or transfer to a plate or bowl.

Contributed by Michele Stahlman

kitchen

Complete in every detail, the Imperial kitchen is easy to clean and keep clean . . . makes meal preparation a pleasure. The double basin sink placed beneath two large windows has a swinging mixing spout, and is available in either a stainless steel or Formica counter top. Plenty of storage space is provided over the stove, above and below the counter top and in the snack bar. The shelf above the snack bar combines beauty and utility. Modern equipment includes an automatic hot water system and an apartment-type gas stove. Twin full-length closets adjoin the 6-cubic-foot electric refrigerator. An efficient ventilating system eliminates excessive heat, smoke and cooking odors.

BLACK BOTTOM CUPCAKES

A delightful combination of rich chocolate cake and creamy cheesecake, these cupcakes are a timeless treat for any occasion.

CREAM CHEESE FILLING

1 (8-ounce) package cream cheese, softened
1 egg
1/2 cup sugar
1/8 teaspoon salt
1 cup semi-sweet chocolate chips

CHOCOLATE CUPCAKES

1 1/2 cups all-purpose flour
1 cup sugar
1/4 cup cocoa powder
1 teaspoon baking soda
1/2 teaspoon salt
1 cup water
1 tablespoon vinegar
1/2 cup vegetable oil
1 teaspoon pure vanilla extract

FOR THE CREAM CHEESE FILLING

1. Preheat your oven to 350 degrees F and line two muffin tins with 24 cupcake liners.

2. Prepare the cream cheese filling by creaming together the softened cream cheese and egg in a medium bowl until smooth. Add the sugar and salt, beating until fully combined. Stir in the chocolate chips and set aside.

FOR THE CHOCOLATE CUPCAKES

1. In a large mixing bowl, combine the flour, sugar, cocoa powder, baking soda, and salt. Mix well, then add the water, vinegar, vegetable oil, and vanilla. Mix until the batter is smooth.

2. Fill each cupcake liner about 1/4 full with the batter, then add a heaping teaspoon of the cream cheese mixture on top of the batter in each cup.

3. Bake for 20 to 25 minutes, or until the cupcakes are set and a toothpick inserted into the chocolate portion comes out clean.

Submitted by Lisa McDonald

CAROLINE'S FOOLPROOF JAM BARS

Whether you're looking for an easy snack to pack up for a long drive or a dessert to share with friends, these bars deliver every time. Sweet and buttery with a touch of fruitiness, they can be made with your favorite preserves. Apricot is the classic choice, but try strawberry, raspberry, or blueberry for a fun twist.

3/4 cup butter, softened
1 cup sugar
1 large egg, room temperature
1/2 teaspoon pure vanilla extract
2 cups all-purpose flour
1/4 teaspoon baking powder
1 1/3 cups sweetened shredded coconut
1/2 cup chopped walnuts
1 (10- to 12-ounce) jar apricot preserves

1. Preheat oven to 350 degrees F. Grease a 9 x 13-inch baking pan and set aside.

2. In a large mixing bowl, cream together the butter and sugar until light and fluffy, about 5 to 7 minutes. Beat in the egg and vanilla.

3. In a separate bowl, whisk together the flour and baking powder. Gradually add the dry ingredients to the creamed mixture, mixing until fully combined.

4. Fold in the shredded coconut and chopped walnuts.

5. Press two-thirds of the dough evenly into the prepared baking pan to form a solid base. Spread the preserves over the dough in an even layer.

6. Crumble the remaining dough over the top of the preserves.

7. Bake for 30 to 35 minutes, or until the top is golden brown. Remove from the oven and cool completely in the pan on a wire rack.

8. Once cool, cut into bars and serve.

TIPS

- *For a nuttier flavor, substitute pecans or almonds for the walnuts.*
- *Sprinkle the top with a light dusting of powdered sugar for an extra touch of sweetness.*
- *These bars freeze well. Wrap them individually for an easy grab-and-go snack.*

Contributed by Caroline Lacitinola

GRACE'S LEMON SQUARES WITH CANDIED LEMON SLICES

These bright and tangy lemon squares are Grace's signature treat—perfect for potlucks, road trips, or a sweet indulgence at home. Topped with beautiful candied lemon slices, they're as stunning as they are delicious.

SHORTBREAD

1/2 cup salted butter, softened*
1/4 cup powdered sugar
1 cup all-purpose flour
Pinch of salt

LEMON FILLING

2 large eggs
1 cup sugar
1/2 teaspoon baking powder
3 tablespoons fresh lemon juice
Zest of 1/2 to 1 lemon
Pinch of salt
3 to 4 tablespoons flour (optional)
Powdered sugar for dusting

CANDIED LEMON SLICES

2 lemons
1 cup water
1 cup granulated sugar

FOR THE SHORTBREAD

1. Preheat your oven to 350 degrees F. Grease and flour an 8 x 8-inch square pan or line it with crinkled parchment paper for easy removal.

2. To make the shortbread, in a medium bowl, beat the butter and powdered sugar together on medium speed until combined and smooth. Add the flour and salt, then beat until a soft dough forms, about 1 1/2 minutes.

Continued →

3. Press the dough evenly into the bottom of the prepared pan. Bake for 18 to 20 minutes, until lightly golden. Remove from the oven and let the base cool completely before adding the filling.

FOR THE FILLING

1. To make the filling, in a medium bowl, whisk together the eggs, sugar, baking powder, lemon juice, lemon zest, and a pinch of salt until smooth. For a thicker filling, mix in 3 to 4 tablespoons flour.

2. Pour the lemon filling evenly over the cooled shortbread base. Return the pan to the oven and bake for 20 to 25 minutes, or until the filling is set and no longer jiggles when gently shaken.

3. Let the lemon bars cool at room temperature for about an hour, then chill in the fridge for 1 to 2 hours for easier slicing. Dust the top with powdered sugar and cut into squares.

FOR THE CANDIED LEMON SLICES

1. To make the candied lemon slices, wash the lemons thoroughly and slice them thinly.

2. Combine water and sugar in a medium saucepan and bring to a boil, stirring until the sugar dissolves.

3. Add the lemon slices to the syrup and simmer on low heat until the slices become translucent, about 30 to 40 minutes.

4. Remove the lemon slices from the syrup and place them on parchment paper to dry for at least 3 hours or overnight.

5. Place the candied lemon slices on top of the lemon squares for an elegant finishing touch.

6. Store in an airtight container in the fridge for up to 4 days. Lemon bars can sit out for a few hours during serving but should return to the fridge for freshness.

**Use unsalted butter with 1/4 teaspoon salt if preferred.*

TIP

- *Lemon squares freeze beautifully. After cooling, arrange the bars on a baking sheet and freeze for an hour. Transfer to a freezer-safe container with parchment paper between layers. Store for up to 3 to 4 months. Dust with powdered sugar after thawing, if desired.*

Contributed by Grace Lacitinola

HARVEST CAMPER FUDGE

This rich and creamy pumpkin fudge is a nostalgic favorite at fall vintage trailer rallies, where its warm spices and sweet, nutty flavors bring everyone together. It's fun to bring to rallies or on camping trips in a vintage tin for a retro touch.

3 cups sugar
3/4 cup butter, softened
1 (5-ounce) can evaporated milk
1/2 cup canned pumpkin puree
1 (10-ounce) package cinnamon chips
1 (7-ounce jar) marshmallow creme
3/4 cup chopped walnuts

1. Line a 9 x 13 x 2-inch baking pan with foil, extending the edges of the foil over the sides. Butter the foil and set aside.

2. In a heavy 3-quart saucepan, combine the sugar, butter, evaporated milk, and pumpkin puree. Cook over medium-high heat, stirring constantly until the mixture begins to boil. Reduce the heat to medium-low and continue cooking and stirring until it reaches the soft-ball stage (230 degrees F) on a candy thermometer, about 20 to 25 minutes.

3. Remove the saucepan from heat. Stir in the cinnamon chips until completely melted and smooth. Add the marshmallow creme and chopped walnuts, mixing until evenly combined.

4. Immediately pour the fudge into the prepared pan and spread evenly with a spatula. While it is still warm, score it into squares with a knife.

5. Allow the fudge to cool completely to room temperature. Once firm, pull on the foil edges to lift it out of the pan. Cut along scored lines into squares.

6. Cover tightly and refrigerate for up to one week. Do not freeze.

TIPS

- *Try swapping pecans for the walnuts or leave the nuts out entirely for a smoother texture.*

- *Substitute chocolate chips for the cinnamon chips. Or, for a unique twist, use a mix of cinnamon and white chocolate chips for a spiced flavor profile.*

Contributed by Carol McRae

SUPER SIMPLE S'MORE BROWNIES

Enjoy these easy, crowd-pleasing treats that bring the campfire to your kitchen!

GRAHAM CRACKER CRUST

1/4 cup butter

5 graham crackers, crushed

BROWNIES

1 boxed brownie mix (plus ingredients required to prepare the mix, such as eggs, oil, and water)

9 jumbo marshmallows, cut in half

FOR THE GRAHAM CRACKER CRUST

1. Preheat your oven to 350 degrees F and line a cupcake pan with paper liners.

2. To make the crust, melt the butter in a large bowl.

3. Crush the graham crackers in a plastic bag until they are fine crumbs.

4. Combine the crumbs with the melted butter and mix well.

5. Add 1 tablespoon of the crust mixture to each cupcake liner. Use an extra liner to press down and form a firm base.

FOR THE BROWNIES

1. Follow the instructions on the boxed brownie mix to prepare the batter.

2. Spoon a heaping tablespoon of brownie batter over each graham cracker crust, filling the liners about 2/3 full.

3. Bake for 15 minutes.

4. After 15 minutes, remove from oven and place half a marshmallow on top of each brownie. Return to oven for an additional 10 minutes.

5. Let the brownies cool completely before serving.

CRISPY MARSHMALLOW SQUARES

This beloved classic has a chewy, gooey texture and nostalgic flavor never fail to please. Whether you're craving something sweet, salty, crunchy, or colorful, these jazzed-up treats are sure to delight everyone, from kids to grown-ups, at your next gathering.

1/4 cup butter
1 (10-ounce) package regular marshmallows or 4 cups of miniature marshmallows
6 cups Rice Krispies® cereal

1. In a large saucepan, melt the butter over low heat.

2. Add the marshmallows and stir continuously until they are completely melted and smooth.

3. Remove the saucepan from heat and gently fold in the Rice Krispies cereal. At this stage, mix in any optional add-ins.

4. Stir until the cereal is evenly coated.

5. Press the mixture into a buttered 9 x 13-inch pan using a buttered spatula or waxed paper.

6. Let the treats cool completely, then cut them into squares.

FUN ADD-INS

- *Mini chocolate chips (mix in after the treats cool slightly to avoid melting)*
- *Cocoa powder mixed into the melted marshmallows*
- *Peanut butter mixed into the melted marshmallow mixture*
- *M&M's or Reese's Pieces*
- *Chopped candy bars such as Snickers, Twix, Reese's peanut butter cups, or KitKat*
- *Crushed Oreos or other sandwich cookies*
- *Mini pretzels or pretzel sticks*
- *Dried cranberries, cherries, or raisins*
- *Candied bacon bits*
- *Caramel-coated or plain popped popcorn*
- *Toasted nuts such as peanuts, almonds, pecans, walnuts, or hazelnuts*

DRIZZLES OR SPRINKLES

- *Melted caramel, chocolate, white chocolate, or butterscotch*
- *Sea salt*
- *Crushed candy canes*

Contributed by Mary Gulley

CAMPFIRE POPCORN

Campfire popcorn is one of those things that turns a regular camping evening into something a little magical. Enjoy experimenting and finding your favorite version.

2 tablespoons cooking oil
1/3 cup popcorn kernels
Salt to taste

1. Let the campfire burn down to hot coals or flames low enough to control.

2. Place a grate over the fire and set a skillet on it.

3. Add oil and 3 to 4 test kernels to skillet. Cover.

4. When the test kernels pop, remove from heat and add the remaining kernels. Cover and return to heat.

5. Shake pan gently and constantly to avoid burning. Once popping slows to 1 to 2 seconds between pops, remove from heat immediately.

6. Let sit a moment (popping may continue). Remove lid very carefully—kernels are hot!

7. Season with salt or try one of the following fun variations.

VARIATIONS

Kettle Corn

1. Add 2 tablespoons sugar to the oil along with the kernels.
2. Stir or shake constantly so sugar doesn't burn.
3. Season lightly with salt after popping.
4. Optional: sprinkle with cinnamon-sugar or a pinch of nutmeg.

Garlic-Parmesan

1/8 cup butter, melted

1/4 cup grated Parmesan

Pinch garlic powder

Pinch Italian seasoning

1. After popping, drizzle popcorn with melted butter.
2. Sprinkle with Parmesan, garlic powder, and Italian seasoning.

RECIPE INDEX

BREAKFAST

MAIN DISHES

FAMILY FAVORITES

ON THE SIDE

DIPS AND SAUCES

WHAT'S FOR DESSERT?

METRIC CONVERSION CHART

Volume Measurements		Weight Measurements		Temperature	
U.S.	Metric	U.S.	Metric	Fahrenheit	Celsius
1 teaspoon	5 ml	1/2 ounce	15 g	250	120
1 tablespoon	15 ml	1 ounce	30 g	300	150
1/4 cup	60 ml	3 ounces	80 g	325	160
1/3 cup	80 ml	4 ounces	115 g	350	175
1/2 cup	125 ml	8 ounces	225 g	375	190
2/3 cup	160 ml	12 ounces	340 g	400	200
3/4 cup	180 ml	1 pound	450 g	425	220
1 cup	250 ml	2 1/4 pounds	1 kg	450	230

TO LIVE IN

AMPLE and efficient refrigeration is provided in the Airfloat. Refrigerator is porcelain and enamel lined. No kneeling down necessary.

Below: A kitchen arranged for comfort and convenience.

ALL Airfloats are equipped with rear disappearing jacks for leveling which provide a firm foundation.

FOR PLEASURE OR BUSINE

THREE MODELS

At left: A compartment entirely separated by sliding doors. As much privacy enjoyed as in your home.

Below: Dinette. Roomy, with convenient window ledge across entire width of coach. Cupboard space below. Windows easily raised from inside.

ABOUT THE AUTHORS

Paul and Caroline Lacitinola are the driving force behind *Vintage Camper Trailers Magazine*, which they've been publishing since 2011. Long before the first issue rolled off the press, they were already immersed in the vintage trailering lifestyle—restoring trailers, hitting the road, and hosting rallies that brought like-minded enthusiasts together. Today, they organize six or more rallies each year, with several drawing more than 250 vintage trailers and the passionate community that surrounds them.

In addition to the magazine, Paul and Caroline have authored two books focused on vintage trailering, *Vintage Camper Trailers* and *Vintage Camper Trailer Rallies,* and continue to champion the hobby through their daily-updated website. Their online platform is a comprehensive resource for rally listings, classified ads, restoration guides, and news from across the trailer community.

Through their events, publications, and hands-on involvement, the Lacitinolas have helped build and sustain one of the most vibrant vintage trailer communities in the United States. This cookbook is a natural extension of their passion—celebrating not only the trailers themselves but also the people, places, and shared meals that make vintage trailering such a rich and rewarding lifestyle.

www.vintagecampertrailers.com